Kundalini Yoga

Secrets to Unlocking Energy, Cleansing Chakras, and Awakening the Shakti within with Kriya

© Copyright 2023 - All rights reserved.

The content contained within this book may not be reproduced, duplicated, or transmitted without direct written permission from the author or the publisher.

Under no circumstances will any blame or legal responsibility be held against the publisher, or author, for any damages, reparation, or monetary loss due to the information contained within this book, either directly or indirectly.

Legal Notice:

This book is copyright protected. It is only for personal use. You cannot amend, distribute, sell, use, quote, or paraphrase any part of the content within this book without the consent of the author or publisher.

Disclaimer Notice:

Please note the information contained within this document is for educational and entertainment purposes only. All effort has been executed to present accurate, up-to-date, reliable, and complete information. No warranties of any kind are declared or implied. Readers acknowledge that the author is not engaging in the rendering of legal, financial, medical, or professional advice. The content within this book has been derived from various sources. Please consult a licensed professional before attempting any techniques outlined in this book.

By reading this document, the reader agrees that under no circumstances is the author responsible for any losses, direct or indirect, that are incurred as a result of the use of the information contained within this document, including, but not limited to, errors, omissions, or inaccuracies.

Your Free Gift
(only available for a limited time)

Thanks for getting this book! If you want to learn more about various spirituality topics, then join Mari Silva's community and get a free guided meditation MP3 for awakening your third eye. This guided meditation mp3 is designed to open and strengthen ones third eye so you can experience a higher state of consciousness. Simply visit the link below the image to get started.

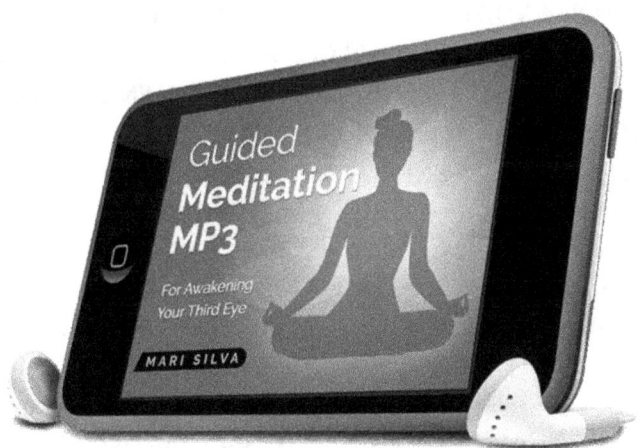

https://spiritualityspot.com/meditation

Table of Contents

INTRODUCTION 1
CHAPTER 1: YOU AND YOUR KUNDALINI SHAKTI 3
CHAPTER 2: GET TO KNOW YOUR CHAKRAS 14
CHAPTER 3: PREPARING THE CHAKRAS FOR THE SNAKE 28
CHAPTER 4: PRANAYAMA AND DRISHTI: FOCUS AND BREATHE 42
CHAPTER 5: UNLOCKING ENERGY WITH MUDRAS AND MANTRAS 52
CHAPTER 6: HOW TO DO KUNDALINI MEDITATION 62
CHAPTER 7: ARAMBHA: A ROOT AWAKENING 72
CHAPTER 8: GHATA: UNLOCKING THE HEART CHAKRA 81
CHAPTER 9: PACIHAYA AND NISHPATTI: UNLOCKING YOUR CROWN 89
CHAPTER 10: KUNDALINI ENERGY IS AWAKENED, NOW WHAT? 97
GLOSSARY OF TERMS 105
CONCLUSION 107
HERE'S ANOTHER BOOK BY MARI SILVA THAT YOU MIGHT LIKE ... 109
YOUR FREE GIFT (ONLY AVAILABLE FOR A LIMITED TIME) 110
REFERENCES 111

Introduction

Have you ever felt the urge to take a deep dive into the mysticism of your being? Kundalini yoga is one way you can do this. It is an ancient spiritual practice that will awaken the dormant energy within your body.

Kundalini yoga is an effective method for connecting with the three elements that make us human, our physical, mental, and spiritual health. Through various meditation tools, breathwork, mudras, mantras, and asanas (yoga poses), the practice focuses on unlocking our potential to open the energy of the seven chakras in the body. Increasing awareness of these channels shows us how to explore the connection between body and mind in our daily lives.

Self-care is vital to a healthy state of mind, body, and spirit. A critical element in caring for ourselves is learning to balance the chakras, the energy centers of our being. As we take time to nurture each one through practices such as yoga, meditation, or visualization, we discover new reserves of self-love. We come to understand that by focusing on inner peace, we can learn to prioritize our holistic health, be kind to ourselves and form healthier connections with the outside world.

Our spirit's journey consists of more than simply our physical body. It is also connected to ethereal energies found in the seven chakras along the spine. We can restore balance in our lives by gaining insight into each one and how it relates to others. Learning about the associated colors, emotions, and mental states related to each chakra helps us become more aware of them so that better alignment can be attained. Understanding how they relate allows us to travel a smoother pathway toward true spiritual enlightenment.

When the Kundalini energy is awakened, it brings awareness of our inner power. A surge of energy is activated, allowing us to reach our full potential and experience a fuller sense of life force. We become more conscious of our physical and spiritual selves, improving our sense of clarity and inner calm. We can then channel this heightened energy into a more focused and conscious state of being.

Regardless of which stage of the Kundalini journey you are at, this book will guide you through this mystical and magical journey. It will take you through the steps of beginning your Kundalini yoga practice. It will explain what to expect, how to prepare, and give tips on maintaining the energy flow for a successful journey. As we go through each chapter, take your time, and explore the depths of your spiritual being. Acknowledge your inner wisdom and use it to guide you. This is an exciting time for personal growth. May your journey be filled with love, light, and peace. Namaste!

Chapter 1: You and Your Kundalini Shakti

Ancient Eastern philosophy has long taught the concept of shakti and Kundalini, a spiritual force complemented by yogic practice. Although these concepts date back centuries, they are becoming increasingly popular in modern-day self-improvement. Through guided meditation and physical exercise, yoga adherents often report mastering a sixth sense and an ability to connect with their inner energy −once solely the domain of spiritual gurus and psychics. Shakti and Kundalini allow those on the journey to enlightenment to reach higher levels of focus, truth, and power within themselves. As such, it is clear why these two ancient concepts remain popular today.

Shakti is a form of divine energy. This is the Hindu depiction of Shakti.
https://www.dollsofindia.com/product/hindu-posters/maa-shakti-encompassing-entire-universe-reprint-on-paper-II99.html, CC BY-SA 4.0 <*https://creativecommons.org/licenses/by-sa/4.0*>, via Wikimedia Commons *https://commons.wikimedia.org/wiki/File:Maa_Shakti.jpg*

This chapter will introduce you to the concept of shakti and Kundalini as it is found in different traditions worldwide. We will first explain the connection between shakti and Kundalini, then explore how they are expressed in various religions, such as Buddhism, Hinduism, Christianity, and even Kabbalistic mysticism or Jungian psychology. Next, we will explore the many benefits of practicing this type of yoga, including physical, mental, and spiritual well-being. This chapter will then go on to discuss what happens when Kundalini is awakened, as well as provide a few real-life accounts. This chapter will also go through each of the four stages of Kundalini awakening and answer any frequently asked questions about it. By the end of this chapter, you'll have a thorough understanding of what shakti and Kundalini are all about.

Introduction to Shakti and Kundalini

Shakti and Kundalini are concepts most often associated with Hinduism and other similar spiritual belief systems. Shakti is a form of divine energy believed to be the source of all creation and enlightenment, while Kundalini is a sleeping coiled energy at the base of each person's spine that must be awakened to reach the highest states of spiritual attainment. Through meditation, movements such as yoga, spiritual practice, and devotion, one can access this powerful energy, which opens the door to unleashing their deeper potential to work towards enlightenment. Once awakened, releasing this power can bring joy, understanding, connection, and direct experience with our true selves.

Shakti, originating from the Hindu tradition, is a feminine divine energy bestowed on all living things at the time of creation. It is often symbolized by different goddesses like Kali and Durga and is believed to bring change into the universe. Shakti radiates power, courage, and willpower associated with motherhood and nurturing qualities. Its cosmic power is transferred through intricate yogic practices and spiritual journeys. Shakti's close connection to Kundalini energy is grounded in its capacity to awaken an individual's internal energy and transform it into powerful energy toward personal enlightenment. Historically, shakti was seen as a way to gain control over one's inner strength. This feeds into the larger societal search for balance between female dominance (grace and compassion) alongside male dominance (physical strength).

The Different Traditions of Kundalini

While sourced from a common set of teachings, several different branches of Kundalini traditions have evolved. From the Sikh tradition in India and its Los Angeles-based offshoot to modern interpretations, this form of spiritual practice has continued to expand and become more accessible worldwide. Each iteration empowers practitioners with unique methods for unlocking their path to higher consciousness, allowing them to explore various aspects of this exciting and rewarding spiritual journey.

A. Buddhism

Founded more than 2,500 years ago in India, the Buddhist tradition contains within it a multifaceted practice of energizing the body and mind. One such practice is that of Kundalini, an ancient meditation discipline focusing on understanding and activating energy stored in the lower spine. By concentrating on energy flows and visualization, practitioners can align their bodies and minds to be open to higher spiritual insights and practical, emotional healing. Kundalini practices have been popular in India for a long time, but they have recently gained popularity in western countries due to advances in yoga science and spiritual studies. It offers an excellent way for people to access the deeper truths of their being, creating a safe place to explore the power of their consciousness.

B. Hinduism

Hinduism is famously known for its wide variety of traditions and rituals, including the Kundalini. This yogic practice is a spiritual rite that works to awaken energy in the body and provide it with heightened awareness and consciousness. It is known that achieving the desired level of Kundalini can lead to greater knowledge and enlightenment. Since believed to be a connection between physical and non-physical energies, it is said that when trained correctly, a person can experience an intense realization of their inner soul. Thus, Kundalini is an essential part of Hindu tradition as it empowers one to open up more dimensions within themselves, ultimately furthering our understanding of spirituality.

C. Christianity

Christianity is an ancient faith that incorporates a multitude of traditions, ranging from a code of ethics to communion and healing. One of the most interesting aspects of Christianity is the tradition of Kundalini, an energetic force associated with the seven chakras, or points of spiritual energy located along the spine. Christian writers have interpreted this as God's living Spirit touching believers through grace. Contemplative practices such as Lectio Divina incorporate Christian principles alongside Kundalini in specifically designed breathing techniques to create powerful experiences for many followers of Christ. Thus, Kundalini is often interwoven into one's practice within modern Christianity as a way to access spiritual awakening and connection with God.

D. Kabbalistic Mysticism

Kabbalistic Mysticism has been practiced for centuries and is based on ancient Jewish mysticism. Its teachings revolve around the idea of using esoteric knowledge and techniques to connect with divinity. The Kundalini tradition is a part of this practice which involves awakening spiritual energies found within every human being to increase self-awareness and potentially reveal the secrets of the universe. It's considered to be a spiritual journey that leads individuals to deeper levels of understanding and connection with something greater than themselves, often through meditative practices such as yoga postures or chanting mantras. The goal of Kabbalistic Mysticism and the tradition of Kundalini are quite different from those associated with other religions. Still, it provides practitioners with a powerful window into the innermost core of their existence, allowing them to experience life on a deeper level.

E. Jungian Psychology

Jungian psychology offers us a unique way of understanding our inner workings through the traditions of Kundalini. This belief is based on the idea of an energy system within the human body, composed of seven major chakras or spiritual power points that work together to bring about wholeness. According to Jungian thought, this energy is activated through an *initiatory experience*, an event or process that forces or allows for a fundamental change in one's life and identity. By engaging with this powerful energy, we can begin to explore ideas like transformation, self-actualization, and reintegration with the unconscious psyche. Through its tradition of utilizing Kundalini, Jungian psychology allows us a more holistic approach to understanding our psyches and working towards wholeness.

Kundalini Yoga

Kundalini Yoga is an ancient practice for spiritual development and self-transformation, using specific kriyas and asanas to help you access your cosmic consciousness. This powerful practice involves connecting with the energy stored within you and in universal consciousness, known as Kundalini. Through focused breathing, meditation, chanting, and other exercises, practitioners of Kundalini Yoga can tap into this powerful force in ways that create physical, mental, and spiritual change.

Kriyas are sets of postures synchronized with the breath to raise or release vital energies, working on the nervous and glandular systems within the body. Asanas are postures designed to increase strength and flexibility while calming the nervous system. Discovering this potent form of yoga will help anyone who integrates its teachings into their daily life experience greater alignment with their true nature.

The Benefits of Kundalini Yoga

With its focus on harnessing the energy and channeling it through poses, breathing techniques, and meditation, Kundalini imparts a range of physical, mental, and spiritual benefits to dedicated practitioners. Physically, Kundalini yoga can improve flexibility, reduce stress, boost metabolism, and increase endurance. On a mental level, it improves concentration, reduces anxiety and depression, and even lifts moods. Those who work with Kundalini have also reported spiritual growth, such as higher states of consciousness, enhanced creativity, and a deep reconnection with their true selves. All these rewards make this traditional practice well worth looking into for anybody looking to deepen their yoga practice or break free from the stresses of modern life.

A. Physical Benefits

One of the major positive spinoffs of Kundalini yoga is stress relief. It's a wonderful way to reduce tension and help restore balance in your body and mind. Kundalini yoga is particularly useful due to its focus on deep breaths and slow, gentle postures/exercises that activate the energy centers throughout the body. This keeps the energy flowing smoothly, reducing stress while increasing flexibility. Over time, regular practice really can change how you feel by improving your energy level overall. With increased flexibility stemming from the physical involvement in the poses and exercises, higher energy levels as a result of improved breathing habits, and reduced stress thanks to targeted breathing techniques, there are many rewards to be gained through Kundalini yoga for those looking for an effective way to cultivate their strength and well-being.

B. Mental Benefits

Practicing Kundalini yoga has several mental benefits, such as promoting clarity of mind, enhancing self-awareness, and improving concentration. Clarity of mind is found through meditative practices like Kundalini Yoga which help by slowing down the mind's inner chatter.

Regular practice reduces feelings of anxiety and stress, replacing them with a more peaceful mindset. Increased self-awareness can help us explore past traumas and easily identify dysfunctional habits. Kundalini's powerful healing mantras can open us up to experience new levels within ourselves we didn't know existed. Lastly, practicing Kundalini Yoga, with its combination of dynamic breathing techniques and vigorous movement, can naturally improve concentration levels without any external tools like medication or supplements. Overall, it's no secret why so many people turn to this form of yoga, as an abundance of mental health-related benefits is associated with it.

C. Spiritual Benefits

Kundalini yoga provides spiritual benefits such as connecting with the divine, gaining wisdom, and accessing higher states of consciousness. When practicing Kundalini yoga, you open yourself up to the divine. You create an inner connection that can be used to explore your beliefs and spirituality. You'll also gain spiritual wisdom while practicing this ancient form of yoga, awakening you to a greater understanding of yourself and life. Finally, Kundalini Yoga can open access to higher states of consciousness that you may not have felt before. It is perfect for those seeking enlightenment or seeking to expand awareness and uncover greater depths within themselves.

Kundalini Awakening: What Happens When It Is Awakened

Kundalini awakening is a complex process that can open up the powerful spiritual life force within. This awakening process can bring physical, emotional, mental, and spiritual transformation. Some of the signs associated with this process are increased intuition, enhanced healing abilities, and improved creativity and focus. Furthermore, Kundalini Awakening can open up spiritual passages to higher levels of consciousness. It has been known to cause the direct experience of psychic powers, clairvoyance, deep insight into your true path in life, and absolute understanding of the cosmic laws of nature. All these possible outcomes make Kundalini Awakening a journey worth taking.

Real-Life Accounts of Kundalini Awakening

Kundalini Awakening, also known as *pranotthana* or *spiritual enlightenment*, is a phenomenon that has been described by many as a life-changing experience. While many people look to religious texts and ancient traditions to understand this state of being, anyone curious about it can find real-life accounts of the event all over the internet. Through interviews, personal journeys, and journal entries, we can see how people came in contact with this spiritual energy and how it changed their lives. Experiences vary from moments of incredible joy and peace right through to an almost overwhelming force that proves difficult to handle. To understand this special moment, nothing replaces hearing stories first-hand from those who went through an authentic Kundalini awakening themselves. Here are some of the most inspiring and enlightening accounts of Kundalini awakenings that we have found:

A. The Awakening of Purna

Purna was a student of yoga who had been studying and practicing for many years. One day she was meditating and felt a sudden surge of energy that was so powerful she wasn't sure if it was an inner experience or something external. She soon realized that this was the awakening of her Kundalini energy. This event transformed Purna into a more intuitive, sensitive, and calm person. She felt connected on a much deeper level with her body, mind, and spirit. Her physical health improved, too, as she no longer suffered from the back pain that had plagued her for years.

B. The Divine Light of David

David was a spiritual seeker who wanted to experience a connection with the divine. As he was meditating one day, he suddenly felt a light enter his body. He said it was like a force of energy that filled him with love, peace, and joy. He experienced a state of clarity and understanding that he had never known before. He described the feeling as an immense power, unlike anything he had ever felt.

C. The Higher Consciousness of Mariel

Mariel was a student of yoga and meditation. She was on a quest to find her true purpose in life when she experienced a powerful Kundalini awakening. She felt an energy that filled her with a deep understanding and connection to the universe. She had what she described as a "profound spiritual revelation," which allowed her to see beyond the physical realm and understand the interconnectedness of all things. Through this experience, Mariel gained a sense of deeper meaning in her life and a greater connection to the spiritual world.

These are just a few of the many real-life accounts out there. While each story is very personal, they all have one thing in common: they illustrate a powerful insight into the potential of Kundalini awakening and the positive transformation it can bring. If you feel called to explore this phenomenon further, many resources are out there to help you on your journey. Don't hesitate to take the leap and explore what spiritual enlightenment can bring to your life.

The Four Stages of Kundalini Awakening

Kundalini awakening consists of a journey of four distinct stages: awakening, cleansing, absorption, and the final stage. During the Awakening stage (Arambha), the spiritual seeker can raise their frequency level to contact their higher self. In the Cleansing stage (Ghata), one goes through processes such as negative feelings, thought patterns, and outmoded beliefs that may be blocking you from connecting more deeply with yourself.

Once this is done, you are ready to move into the Absorption stage (*Pacihaya*), where you can become fully aware of your higher self and manifest your true desires. Lastly, in the Final stage (Nishpatti), the integration of all aspects of self fully leads one to complete illumination and enlightenment. The practice of Kundalini awakening is a powerful tool for those who seek inner peace and transformation.

While the process can be challenging, the rewards are great. Those who embark on this path will find themselves changed profoundly and with a greater sense of connection to their higher self. Regardless of which stage you are at in your spiritual journey, Kundalini awakening can be a powerful tool to help you reach the next level.

FAQs

While Kundalini awakenings can be a deeply spiritual and personal experience, many people have questions about the process. Here are some of the most common FAQs about Kundalini awakenings and the stages of spiritual transformation.

Q: Is It Dangerous?

A: Kundalini awakenings are not in and of themselves dangerous. However, it is crucial to be mindful of the intensity of the energy as it can be overwhelming and potentially negatively impacts one's physical, mental, and emotional health. Working with an experienced teacher or practitioner who can support and guide you through the process is essential.

Q: Is Kundalini Awakening Difficult?

A: Every Kundalini awakening is unique and can vary in difficulty. It depends on the individual's level of spiritual practice, emotional and physical health, and comfort level with the process. It is a transformative journey and requires patience, practice, and dedication. You should work with a teacher or practitioner who can provide guidance and support.

Q: How Long Does the Process Take?

A: Kundalini awakenings can take anywhere from a few weeks to several years. It is essential to be patient and to trust in the process. By working alongside a certified teacher or practitioner, you can ensure your journey is safe and successful. It is also crucial to be mindful of one's emotional and physical well-being to ensure the journey is healthy and beneficial.

Q: Can Anyone Awaken Their Kundalini?

A: Kundalini awakenings are available to all individuals who are willing to embark on the journey. It is crucial, however, to be mindful of one's physical, mental, and emotional health before beginning the process. You should also work with an experienced teacher or practitioner who can provide guidance and support throughout the process.

Q. Is It Worth Pursuing?

A: If you seek a spiritual path of greater inner knowledge and connection to the divine, then Kundalini awakening can be incredibly rewarding. It can bring intense clarity, greater purpose, and a profound sense of knowing. With patience and dedication, the process can offer tremendous insight and transformation that can be deeply meaningful and beneficial.

Kundalini awakening is a powerful opportunity for spiritual transformation, self-discovery, and connection with the divine. It is an ancient practice used for centuries to help seekers gain inner knowledge, peace, and transformation. By understanding the stages of spiritual transformation, the potential risks and benefits of Kundalini awakenings, and the importance of working with an experienced teacher, you can ensure that your journey is safe and successful.

Chapter 2: Get to Know Your Chakras

Kundalini awakening is an ancient yogic practice that countless masters have tapped into over the centuries. It is essentially a way to unleash the hidden, untapped potential within each of us. Kundalini awakening first requires settling and calming the mind so that our inner force can be revealed in its purest form. Once we connect with our Kundalini (also known as life force energy), we open ourselves up to heightened consciousness and spiritual transformations. This allows us to experience higher levels of awareness and perception than ever before.

In unlocking the dormant power available via Kundalini, we connect with ourselves on an entirely new level. It is a sacred practice that has existed since the dawn of time. The chakras play a pivotal role in the Kundalini process, as they are the energy centers that the awakened energy will "slither" through on its journey up the spine. This chapter will act as a general presentation of the chakras and their connection with the Kundalini energy. It will illustrate the chakra's symbol, Sanskrit name, and its location and role in the system. It will cover each chakra's color, sound, and mantra. We'll also explore blockage symptoms and clear chakra sensations which can be experienced when the chakras are open.

Introduction to the Chakras

The chakras are ancient Indian energy centers that have long been associated with physical, mental, and spiritual well-being. Each of the seven main chakras located along the spine corresponds to different states of consciousness and is believed to influence how we take in the process and express life's energy. To help balance our energetic system, we can use various tools such as affirmations, breathing techniques, visualizations, sound healing, and yoga to open the flow of energy through each chakra and awaken a more mindful connection with our inner selves. Understanding how these powerful energy centers interact with us in unique ways and how we can facilitate their natural flow of life force will help us ultimately achieve our highest potential.

Muladhara: The Root Chakra

The Muladhara, the root chakra, serves as the foundation of the human body's energy system. This base-level energetic center helps fuel our physical and emotional well-being by drawing energy from the earth and providing a power source for our lives. The associated element to this chakra is earth, so grounding ourselves is key for keeping this chakra balanced and active. When feeling ungrounded or disrupted in balance, one can reconnect with their root chakra through activities such as yoga, dancing, or meditating outdoors or on the ground. This allows us to remain centered and at peace within our skin.

The root chakra.
https://pixabay.com/es/illustrations/chakra-mandala-chakra-ra%c3%adz-1340058/

A. Symbol and Sanskrit Name

The symbol associated with the root chakra is a four-petaled lotus flower that sits atop a square. The Sanskrit name for this chakra is Muladhara, which translates to "root support" or "base."

B. Location and Role

Muladhara can be found at the base of the spine. It is associated with safety, security, and stability. It is a grounding chakra, which means that it keeps us connected with reality and allows us to have balanced physical energy. Emotionally, Muladhara provides us with feelings of security and trust in ourselves and our environment. Physically, this chakra's balanced energy gives us good posture, strong immunity, and balanced metabolism. Activating this energy center also makes it easier for people to manifest their desires as it increases their ability to stay focused on their goals.

C. Color, Sound, and Mantra

The Muladhara is the foundation for the entire energetic system in the body. Represented by a deep red color and a steady drumbeat, its energy is focused on feeling secure and grounded in our environment. The root chakra can be aligned with meditation involving mantras repeated silently to oneself, such as "I am safe." This mantra helps to open and balance the energetic state of mind allowing for higher levels of well-being.

D. Blockage Symptoms

When we experience a blockage to this chakra, it can manifest in many physical, mental, and emotional symptoms. Low energy, insecurity, feeling disconnected from others, and difficulty grounding yourself are some common signs of imbalance. Digestive problems or accidents can indicate that our root chakra needs attention and should not be ignored. Clearing out any stagnant energy from this chakra will restore balance to your overall well-being and make you feel secure.

E. Clear Chakra Sensations

When experiencing a clear Muladhara, you may feel lighter in your body, as if the weight on your shoulders has been lifted. You may also feel more grounded and connected to the earth, with a strong sense of stability and security. Physically, your digestive system might work better, releasing stagnant energy and helping you digest food more effectively. Mentally, a clear root chakra can help you feel less stressed and overwhelmed by everyday life. Furthermore, a balanced root chakra helps us accept our intuition and have faith in the unknown. All these effects result from unlocking an open chakra, which allows us to tap into inner strength and connect with our true selves.

Svadhisthana: The Sacral Chakra

The Sacral Chakra is associated with emotion and creativity and helps to process our physical and emotional experiences. This chakra regulates our feelings of pleasure, sensuality, and relationships with ourselves and others. When this chakra is balanced, we can relate to life from a place of joy instead of fear or guilt. Free-flowing energy in this area allows us to let go of expectations or self-judgment, enabling us to move joyfully through life's challenges and accept what it offers us. Practicing yoga poses that focus on alignment, breath work, and grounding activities (like journaling) can help restore harmony in the sacral chakra so we can experience life with an open heart.

The sacral chakra.
https://pixabay.com/es/illustrations/naranja-chakra-mandala-svadhisthana-1340073/

A. Symbol and Sanskrit Name

The *Svadhisthana* in Sanskrit, or "sacral chakra, is located on the pelvic floor and is represented by a lotus flower with six orange petals. This chakra's energy controls creativity, relationships, sex drive, and emotions such as pleasure and sensuality. It encourages you to accept and explore yourself and your passions without judgment. Harnessing this chakra's power has many proven health benefits, including improved mental clarity and emotional balance.

B. Location and Role

Svadhisthana, one of the seven primary chakras associated with Hindu and Buddhist practices, is also known as the sacral chakra. It is located below the naval, just above the pelvic area. It is mostly connected to relationships and sexuality. However, it can be used in so much more. Svadhisthana is known to bring creativity and joy when opened up properly. People can use its powers for emotional intelligence, healing from trauma, and connecting with physical sensibilities (taste, smell, touch). To tap into this positivity, one must learn to meditate on this energetic center to open themselves up emotionally and be mindful of their decisions. Then they can truly benefit from Svadhishthana's wisdom.

C. Color, Sound, and Mantra

Svadhisthana is associated with the color orange, the sound "Vam," and the mantra "I Feel." Svadhisthana represents our emotional life and sexual energy. Working with this chakra allows us to tap into our creativity, express ourselves more freely, and access greater spiritual abundance. Embracing our creative potential encourages us to take risks and find the courage within. Inviting in the orange hue of Svadhisthana supports feelings of pleasure and flow as we work towards living authentically!

D. Blockage Symptoms

When this chakra is blocked or imbalanced, we may experience a feeling of disconnection with our bodies or emotions. Along with physical sensations such as pain in the groin or lower back area, you may feel insecure or lack trust in yourself or others. You may also have difficulty relating to relationships on an emotional level. Low energy levels, feelings of being stuck in life, and general apathy towards activities that would normally be enjoyable could be signs that you have a blockage in your Svadhisthana chakra.

E. Clear Chakra Sensations

When this chakra is balanced, we feel free from emotion's grip as our body fills with pleasurable sensations. On the other hand, when it is blocked or unbalanced, we experience negative emotions such as jealousy and insecurity that arise in our inner waters. Opening this chakra allows us to explore our creative side without fear and increase pleasure through natural expression. Achieving balance starts with becoming aware of your feelings and understanding yourself. Regular exercise and yoga can help you clear pathways and open up energy flow to create a state of harmony.

Manipura: The Solar Plexus Chakra

Manipura, or the solar plexus chakra, is one of seven chakras in the human body and is associated with self-empowerment and purpose. Many spiritualists believe that it is the core center of willpower and strength. Tapping into Manipura serves as a turbo boost for our mental and physical vitality. Working on this chakra can help us approach life with enthusiasm, drive, clarity, and confidence. Meditation allows us to access these powerful qualities within ourselves; drawing out the unique energy found in Manipura with each breath can be particularly effective. As we commit to unblocking our solar plexus chakra, we make progress toward unlocking our true potential!

The solar plexus chakra.
https://pixabay.com/es/illustrations/mandala-chakra-del-plexo-solar-1340066/

A. Symbol and Sanskrit Name

Manipura is represented by a downward-pointing triangle, symbolizing our innate power and the fire from within. Its Sanskrit name means "lustrous gem;" it is located in the solar plexus.

B. Role and Benefits

Manipura serves as a great source of power in our lives. It is the gateway to manifesting our dreams and aspirations through action. When its energy is balanced, we experience an increase in self-confidence, a greater ability to make decisions and feel empowered. We can also enhance our physical energy, strengthen our digestion, and increase our ability to take on challenging tasks.

C. Color, Sound, and Mantra

Manipura is associated with the color yellow and the sound "Ram." Its mantra is "I Do." Working with the vibration of this chakra can help us move forward in our lives and take control of our destinies.

D. Blockage Symptoms

When this chakra is blocked or out of balance, we tend to feel emotionally and physically sluggish. Low levels of energy, difficulty making decisions, feelings of insecurity, and an inability to take risks are all signs that work is needed to clear blockages in your Manipura chakra. Other common physical symptoms of a blocked Manipura include digestive issues, fatigue, and aches in the upper body.

E. Clear Chakra Sensations

When Manipura is balanced, we experience a surge of energy that allows us to move through life with direction and purpose. We can confidently make decisions, trust our intuition, and leap into unknown territory. To open this chakra, practice yoga and meditate on working with its mantra "I Do." Feel empowered and free as you unlock the potential of your solar plexus chakra!

Anahata: The Heart Chakra

The Anahata, or heart chakra, is one of the seven primary chakras of the human energy system. It relates to matters of compassion, love, and emotional balance in our lives. Through building this chakra's energy, we can learn to integrate these qualities into our lives as tools for personal growth. Working with the Anahata implies being in touch with all other chakras and understanding their relationship to create a healthy state of being. Therapeutic practices such as meditation and yoga are among the suggested forms of developing Anahata's energy, offering insight into how to access more heartfelt emotions. With mindfulness practices related to this energy center, we cultivate inner peace and feelings of unconditional love for both ourselves and others.

The heart chakra.
https://pixabay.com/es/illustrations/verde-anahata-chakra-del-coraz%c3%b3n-1340075/

A. Symbol and Sanskrit Name

Anahata is represented by a lotus flower with twelve petals, signifying its connection to the heart. Its Sanskrit name means "unhurt" and is in the center of the chest.

B. Role and Benefits

Anahata bridges our physical and spiritual bodies, allowing us to connect with our higher self. When its energy is balanced, we experience increased compassion, self-love, and the ability to forgive and accept. We can also enhance our creativity and emotional intelligence, increase our capacity for empathy, and build strong relationships.

C. Color, Sound, and Mantra

Anahata is associated with the color green and the sound "Yam." Its mantra is "I Love." Working with this chakra vibration can help us open our hearts and cultivate feelings of love, acceptance, and compassion.

D. Blockage Symptoms

When this chakra is blocked or out of balance, we tend to feel emotionally disconnected from others and find it hard to trust in relationships. Feelings of loneliness, fear of intimacy, and difficulty expressing emotions are all signs that you may need to work on clearing some blockages in your Anahata chakra. Other common physical symptoms of a blocked Anahata include heart palpitations, chest pain, and immune system issues.

E. Clear Chakra Sensations

When Anahata is balanced, we experience a sense of inner peace and contentment. We can accept our own emotions, as well as those of others, without judgment or fear. To open this chakra, practice yoga and meditation on working with its mantra, "I Love." Feel the love that radiates from your heart, the unconditional love you have for yourself and others!

Vishuddha: The Throat Chakra

The throat chakra is one of seven major energy centers within the body, known as Vishuddha. Its relevance and importance lie in its ability to open our vocal cords and express truth and creativity. With energy flowing freely through this chakra, we can harness our power of communication. This can improve our relationships with ourselves and others and help us develop clarity and speak confidently. When we can release the blockages of this chakra, we become more expressive and more open-minded toward new ideas and perspectives. The openness of the Vishuddha Chakra can help us accept what comes our way throughout life's journey with a light heart and better outcomes.

The throat chakra.
https://pixabay.com/es/illustrations/azul-claro-vishuddha-chakra-mandala-1340078/

A. Symbol and Sanskrit Name

Vishuddha is the Sanskrit name for the throat chakra and is represented by a sixteen-petaled lotus flower. Its Sanskrit name translates to "purification," and it is located at the base of the throat.

B. Role and Benefits

The Vishuddha chakra governs our way of speaking, thinking, listening, and communicating with others. We can express ourselves with clarity and confidence when its energy is balanced. It also helps us to stay open-minded about new ideas and perspectives. Other benefits include improved relationships, better communication, and an overall increase in self-confidence.

C. Color, Sound, and Mantra

Vishuddha is associated with the color blue and the sound "Ham." Its mantra is "I Speak." Practicing this mantra will help to open up your throat chakra and release blockages.

D. Blockage Symptoms

When Vishuddha is blocked or out of balance, we may feel like our communication is stifled and restricted. We can also experience difficulty in speaking the truth and expressing our opinions, as well as having difficulty in listening to others. Physical symptoms of blockages can include throat pain, neck tension, and laryngitis.

E. Clear Chakra Sensations

When Vishuddha is balanced, we feel more open and receptive toward others' ideas and perspectives. We can easily express ourselves confidently and clearly. To open this chakra, practice yoga postures that focus on stretching the neck and throat area. However, the most crucial step is to work on releasing any unexpressed emotions or thoughts you may be holding onto. Acknowledge them and allow yourself to express your truth without fear.

Ajna: The Third Eye Chakra

Ajna is a vital energy point in many yogic practices, commonly called the *third eye chakra*. It is traditionally believed to open up one's psychic potential and sharpen intuition and inner knowledge. When balanced, this chakra can lead to a higher perception and understanding of ourselves, our relationships, and the world around us. To balance this particular energy point, it's essential to focus on cultivating clarity and trusting our wisdom. Through breath work, meditation, and self-reflection, we can begin to understand how we process and interpret information through Ajna's pathway for spiritual growth. Once opened, it allows for a true merger in deeper meditation states. The unspoken messages are heard clearly in the individual's consciousness.

The third eye chakra.
https://pixabay.com/es/illustrations/azul-chakra-mandala-meditaci%c3%b3n-1340076/

A. Symbol and Sanskrit Name

A two-petaled lotus flower represents *Ajna*. Its Sanskrit name translates to "command" or "perception," and it is located between the eyebrows.

B. Role and Benefits

The Ajna Chakra governs our intuition, imagination, wisdom, and perception of truth. When its energy is balanced, we can access a higher level of understanding and clarity. It helps us to connect with our inner knowledge and tap into our psychic potential. Benefits include improved intuition, better decision-making, creativity, and sharper concentration.

C. Color, Sound, and Mantra

Ajna is associated with the color indigo and the sound "Aum." Its mantra is "I See." Practicing this mantra will help to open up your third eye chakra and release blockages.

D. Blockage Symptoms

When Ajna is blocked or out of balance, we may have difficulty understanding our intuition and trusting our inner wisdom. We can also feel disconnected from our spiritual paths and find it hard to focus on the bigger picture. Physical symptoms of blockages can include tension headaches, fatigue, and difficulty in making decisions.

E. Clear Chakra Sensations

When Ajna is balanced, we have greater clarity and understanding of ourselves and others. We become more intuitive and can make decisions with confidence. To open this chakra, practice yoga postures focusing on the area between the eyebrows or a gentle head massage to help soothe any tension. Develop your inner wisdom and trust yourself by listening to your intuition; this will provide a solid foundation for understanding the deeper layers of Ajna.

Sahasrara: The Crown Chakra

The crown chakra is the highest energy point in the body and is located right at the top of the head. Known as *Sahasrara*, it represents enlightenment, spiritual connection, and our higher self. When opened, we can access a higher level of consciousness and experience a deeper connection to our spiritual nature.

The crown chakra.
https://pixabay.com/es/illustrations/violeta-blanco-chakra-1340083/

A. Symbol and Sanskrit Name

A thousand-petaled lotus flower represents *Sahasrara*; its Sanskrit name translates to "thousandfold" or "limitless." It is located at the top of the head and symbolizes enlightenment and spiritual connection.

B. Role and Benefits

The crown chakra is the highest energy point in the body and governs our spirituality, understanding of ourselves, and our connection with a higher power. When balanced, it helps us to connect deeply with our inner wisdom and access higher levels of consciousness. Benefits include improved intuition, greater clarity, enhanced creativity, and spiritual connection.

C. Color and Sound

Sahasrara is associated with purple or white and the sound "Aum." Its mantra is "I See." Repeating this mantra will help to open up your crown chakra and release any blockages you may be experiencing.

D. Blockage Symptoms

When the crown chakra is blocked or out of balance, we can experience feelings of disconnection from our spiritual paths and a lack of direction in life. We may feel disconnected from our higher power or have difficulty trusting our inner wisdom. Physical symptoms of blockages can include insomnia, headaches, and mental fatigue.

E. Clear Chakra Sensations

When the crown chakra is balanced, we feel connected to a higher power and have an overall clarity of our spiritual purpose. To open this chakra, practice yoga postures focusing on the top of the head or gently massage. Spend some time in nature and connect with your surroundings, opening up the crown chakra and providing a spiritual connection.

We can access our inner wisdom that can guide us through life by harnessing and understanding the chakras' power. Working on balancing each of the chakras will help to bring harmony into our lives and tap into our full potential. It is a lifelong journey of self-discovery and spiritual growth.

The practice of awakening and balancing the chakras through yoga, meditation, massage, and other holistic healing modalities can help to bring balance into our lives, reduce stress levels, and help us to reach our highest potential. Understanding the chakras' power allows us to access our inner wisdom that can guide us through life. With practice, we can awaken and balance the energy of each chakra to achieve a state of harmony and well-being.

By understanding the roles of the various chakras, we learn how to open them up and harness their power for greater spiritual growth. We must begin by understanding the power of the Kundalini energy and how it affects each chakra and its associated roles. By awakening this energy, we open ourselves to a new world of spiritual exploration and growth.

Once we understand each chakra's role in our lives, we can begin to explore ways to awaken and balance the energy of each chakra to achieve a state of harmony and well-being!

Chapter 3: Preparing the Chakras for the Snake

The chakras are powerful energy centers, each governing different parts of our physical, mental, and emotional well-being. When out of balance or blocked, they can lead to a range of issues. Keeping your chakras balanced and healthy is essential to experiencing a sense of well-being and maintaining emotional, mental, and spiritual equilibrium. To ensure this balance, it is necessary to regularly cleanse and unblock your chakras. Regular cleansing removes negative energy and allows positive energy to flow freely. Unblocking the chakras ensures that the energy pathways remain open so that energy can continuously circulate through all seven centers in the body.

Preparing the chakras for cleansing and unblocking is a critical part of the process. This can be done through disciplines such as meditation, breathwork, mantras, visualization, yoga, or other physical activity. This chapter will guide you through how to cleanse and unblock each chakra. Following the methods outlined here, you can balance your chakras and align with your highest self.

Opening the Root Chakra

The root chakra is a powerful energy point found at the base of the spine and serves as a grounding force in all aspects of life. Opening the root chakra clears any energetic blocks that might be present and re-aligns our inner connection toward stability, security, and balance. It allows any emotions that may have been pushed away or suppressed to *rise*. Ultimately, this helps us to better connect with our bodies and have open conversations about what we need to feel secure and grounded. Working with this chakra can improve resilience, strength, and creativity, making it integral for those looking for an overall feeling of healthiness on their journey of self-discovery.

Diet Advice/Detox

Root chakra detoxing focuses on providing stability and a feeling of being grounded both emotionally and in life. Several simple diet tips can help you open this vital energy center in your body.

- Start by adding more root vegetables to your diet, like potatoes, carrots, onions, and sweet potatoes.
- Including warming spices such as cumin and cardamom is another dietary addition to help stimulate the root chakra's energetic flow.
- Eating freshly prepared meals that are nutrient-rich and starting with a healthy base of vegetables will help to provide the foundation for a balanced root chakra.

Lifestyle Changes

Making conscious changes to your lifestyle can positively affect your emotional and physical health, particularly when it comes to opening the root chakra. Some simple ways to promote root chakra health include:

- Spending more time outdoors
- Staying connected with people you trust
- Eating naturally nutritious foods
- Engaging in physical activities you enjoy
- Setting healthy boundaries
- Allowing yourself time for rest.

Taking care of ourselves creates a ripple effect that can help us face personal and professional challenges with greater resiliency. Nothing can be gained from overworking or getting stuck in unhealthy behaviors. Making these adjustments can be challenging initially, but committing to a healthier lifestyle is an invaluable opportunity for self-growth and development.

Asanas/Yoga Poses

Opening the root chakra through yoga postures can be powerful and effective. One of the best ways to begin is by standing flat on the floor and getting into the mountain pose. This simple asana grounds you and establishes your connection with the physical world, creating a foundation of awareness. From there, you can explore postures like squats and forward folds, keeping the knees soft and conscious, focusing on connecting with your breath. Seated postures that stretch and massage along the spine, such as those found in cat-cow, can also help open up your feeling of belonging in physical space.

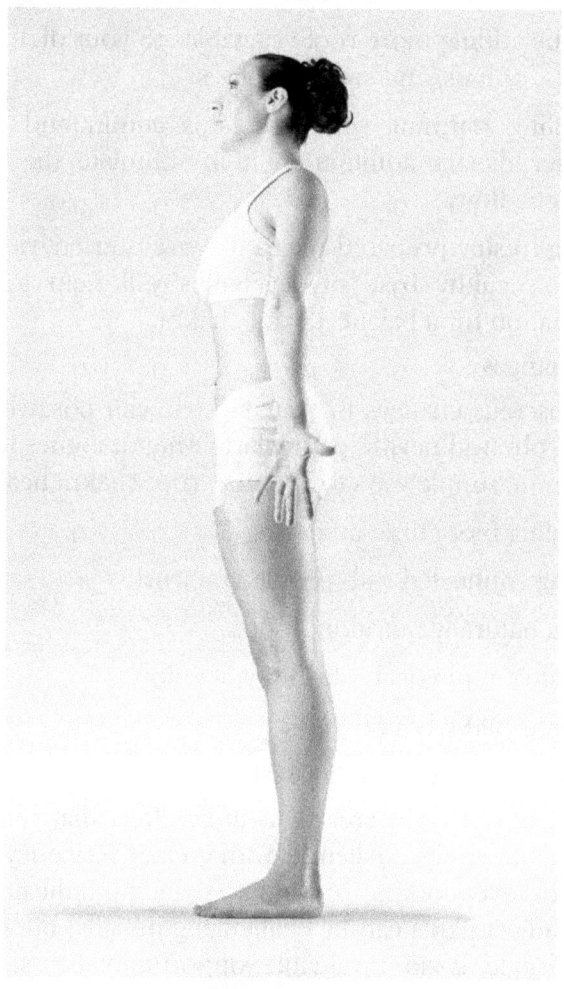

Mountain pose.
https://commons.wikimedia.org/wiki/File:Mr-yoga-mountain-pose-1.jpg

Cleansing the Sacral Chakra

Cleansing the sacral chakra is a powerful way to unlock creativity, passion, and sensuality in your life. It is essential for ushering in emotion-driven activities that can deepen relationships and calm anxieties about responsibility. Practicing self-reflection is a great way to start any journey toward cleansing this chakra. This can be done by journaling or meditating on who you are, the kind of life you want to lead, and how your values relate to it. Regular physical activities such as yoga or dance can open up blocked energies around this area in our bodies. Finally, listening to music, painting, and decorating with bright colors all help to enhance the connection we have with ourselves and others, allowing creative energy to flow more freely.

Diet Advice/Detox

In terms of dietary advice, sacral chakra detoxing requires plenty of hydration. Drinking enough water allows the body to flush out toxins and remain properly hydrated. Here are some other sacral chakra-friendly dietary tips:

- Increase your intake of oranges and other citrus fruits containing Vitamin C.
- Include foods that are high in antioxidants, such as blueberries and dark chocolate.
- Consume more omega-3 fatty acids found in salmon, flaxseed, and walnuts.
- Eating foods rich in magnesium and calcium, like leafy greens, bananas, nuts, and seeds, can help to further balance the sacral chakra.

Lifestyle Changes

Making conscious lifestyle changes, such as prioritizing self-care and allowing yourself to explore different creative outlets, can be a great way to get the sacral chakra moving. Taking time out from a hectic schedule to simply relax can be incredibly helpful in getting yourself to connect with your emotions on a deeper level. Here are some other great lifestyle tips for activating the sacral chakra:

- Take a bath or shower in Epsom salts to create an atmosphere of peace and relaxation.

- Engage in activities that bring joy and pleasure, such as walking outdoors or listening to music.
- Explore new creative projects and make time for hobbies that you truly enjoy.
- Create a supportive environment by surrounding yourself with positive and uplifting people.

Asanas/Yoga Poses

When it comes to finding the right poses for opening up the sacral chakra, focus on postures that stretch and massage along the lower back and hips. Forward folds are especially beneficial, as they can help to release tension in the body that has been blocked from lack of movement. The goddess pose is one of the best poses for this chakra, as it simultaneously opens up both the hips and the sacral area. Supported bridge and fire log poses are also excellent postures for stimulating the sacral chakra.

Goddess pose.
https://pixahive.com/photo/utka%E1%B9%ADa-ko%E1%B9%87asana-goddess-pose/

Unblocking the Solar Plexus Chakra

Our solar plexus chakra is the energy center in our bodies that greatly impacts how we feel. When blocked, we can be overwhelmed with fear, self-doubt, and anxiety, making it hard to face our inner truth. There are many ways to unblock this chakra, like meditation and yoga, but sometimes we need more of an abundance mindset shift by recognizing the good things in life and doing the things that make us happy. Pursuing positive thinking, maintaining healthy relationships, and actively practicing self-love assists us in reclaiming our power and opens us up to new opportunities – helping us shine from the inside out.

Diet Advice/Detox

When it comes to cleansing this chakra, the best advice is to flush out toxins. Start by drinking plenty of water to stay hydrated and flush out the gut. Eating plenty of fruits and vegetables while reducing your intake of processed foods can help to increase energy and improve digestion. Here are some other dietary tips to consider:

- Include more leafy greens in your meals, such as spinach and kale.
- Increase your intake of high-fiber foods like oats and brown rice.
- Snack on seeds, nuts, and legumes such as lentils or chickpeas.
- Eating lighter, more organic meals that contain healing spices like turmeric can also be beneficial.

Lifestyle Changes

Making lifestyle changes focusing on self-care and positive thinking can also help unblock the solar plexus chakra. Connecting with nature by taking a walk in the park or simply soaking up some sunshine can be incredibly relaxing and help balance this chakra. Here are some other lifestyle tips to consider:

- Look out for positive affirmations and mantras that resonate with you.
- Take up a hobby or activity that you find enjoyable, such as painting or baking.
- Forgive yourself and others for any mistakes made in the past.
- Practicing yoga, meditation, and deep breathing exercises can be incredibly beneficial.

Asanas/Yoga Poses

When finding the right poses for opening up the solar plexus chakra, focus on energizing and uplifting postures. Sun salutations are an excellent choice, as they help awaken the body and stir energy from within. Standing poses stretching the spine and opening up the chest, such as warrior I and II, are also great for this chakra. Boat pose, bow pose, and upward facing dog can help to increase flexibility and give the midsection a gentle massage. Finally, the corpse pose is helpful for creating mindfulness and giving your body a chance to relax and recharge.

Sun salutation.
https://commons.wikimedia.org/wiki/File:Mr-yoga-sun_salutation_1.jpg

Rebalancing the Heart Chakra

Healing and rebalancing the heart chakra requires patience, awareness, and commitment. The fourth chakra is the bridge between our physical world and spiritual self. Connecting these two aspects of our being brings balance to daily life, which is necessary for overall health and well-being. To open the heart chakra, mindfulness is an essential element. Focus on love and compassion for oneself and others, express emotions freely, act out of kindness, and incorporate yoga postures that stimulate energy flow through the heart. Each of these processes connects with our inner truth to heal any blockages or traumas that prevent us from fully expressing ourselves.

Diet Advice/Detox

To open the heart chakra, focusing on detoxing and nourishing the body is beneficial. While it is crucial to maintain a healthy diet, certain foods can help with cleansing and opening the heart chakra. Here are a few tips to consider:

- Increase your intake of whole grains, such as quinoa and buckwheat.
- Include lots of leafy greens such as spinach, kale, and Swiss chard.
- Including more green vegetables in your diet, such as broccoli and spinach, can help to promote detoxification.
- Eat foods that are rich in antioxidants, like berries or dark chocolate.

Lifestyle Changes

Making lifestyle changes that focus on self-love and kindness can help to unblock the heart chakra. It is important to practice compassion and forgive oneself and others. Here are some helpful tips to consider:

- Engage in activities that make you feel connected with yourself, such as journaling and meditation.
- Surround yourself with people that make you feel valued and appreciated.
- Do something nice for someone else, even if it's something small.
- Take time for yourself and do things that make you feel happy and relaxed, such as listening to music or going for a walk.

Asanas/Yoga Poses

When it comes to finding the right poses for opening up the heart chakra, focus on cleansing and calming postures. Heart openers such as cobra, wheel, and bridge pose can stir up energy in the chest and awaken the heart. Backbends such as upward bow pose, camel, and bow pose can create a strong connection between the heart and back body. Finally, gentle inversions such as supported shoulder stands, legs up the wall, and fish poses are all beneficial for releasing tension from the chest and inviting harmony into the heart.

Cobra pose.
https://pixahive.com/photo/cobra-pose-bhujangasana/

Purifying the Throat Chakra

The throat chakra, also known as the Vishuddha, is represented by the color blue and governs communication and self-expression. When this area of our being is unbalanced or "clogged," our ability to express ourselves honestly and confidently may be blocked. To purify your throat chakra, it is best to commit to a daily practice of vocalizing mantras, affirmations, or simply saying out loud things that you need to express but are afraid to. Doing this, even for a few minutes each day, can help identify areas in which communication needs healing in your life so that you may be able to work towards achieving a full balance within your throat chakra.

Diet Advice/Detox

The throat chakra is connected with the thyroid gland, which is responsible for regulating metabolism and energy levels. Eating foods that are beneficial to both the throat and the thyroid can be helpful in cleansing and opening the throat chakra. Here are a few tips to consider:

- Increase your intake of iodine-rich foods such as seaweed, eggs, and seafood.
- Include plenty of water-rich foods like cucumbers, celery, and melons.
- Eat foods that are high in antioxidants.

Lifestyle Changes

In addition to diet, lifestyle changes can also open and cleanse the throat chakra. Here are some helpful tips to consider:

- Take time for creative outlets, such as writing or music, to help you express yourself and your feelings.
- Make a conscious effort to be mindful of the words that come out of your mouth and practice speaking truthfully, without judgment.
- Get in touch with your spiritual side and meditate or practice yoga to help open up the throat chakra.

Asanas/Yoga Poses

When it comes to finding the right poses for opening up the throat chakra, focus on gentle and calming postures. Neck openers such as cat/cow, shoulder stand, and fish pose can help to release tension from the neck area, which is connected to the throat chakra. Backbends such as bow, camel, and cobra pose can create space in the chest area and awaken the throat chakra. Inversions such as a supported shoulder stand and legs up the wall can also balance the throat chakra by providing a sense of comfort and peace. Finally, supine twisting poses such as half lord of the fishes and revolved triangle can purify and open the throat chakra.

Fish pose.
Mr. Yoga, CC BY-SA 4.0 <https://creativecommons.org/licenses/by-sa/4.0/deed.en> via Wikimedia Commons https://commons.wikimedia.org/wiki/File:Mr-yoga-fish-pose.jpg

Illuminating the Third Eye Chakra

Many people turn to the illumination of their third eye chakra as an essential step in strengthening themselves spiritually. By tapping into the energies associated with this area, one can find greater insight, balance, and clarity in their life. It is believed that accessing this energy center boosts intuition and opens us up to experiencing our true potential. With regular meditation, deep relaxation (or even visualizing a bright white light in the center of our forehead), we can slowly but surely start to become aware of what lies behind our physical body on a spiritual level. Ultimately, these techniques are powerful tools for connecting to our inner wisdom, which takes us on a journey of self-discovery and transformation.

Diet Advice/Detox

As the third eye chakra is associated with sight, eating foods that are good for our eyesight can cleanse and open this area of our being. To open the third eye chakra, try to eat foods high in Vitamin A, such as carrots and spinach. In addition, try to limit your intake of processed or sugary food as these can damage our eyesight. Here are some helpful tips to consider:

- Increase your intake of Vitamin A-rich foods such as carrots, spinach, and sweet potatoes.
- Avoid processed or sugary foods.
- Eat plenty of dark leafy greens such as kale, arugula, and collards.

Lifestyle Changes

Certain lifestyle changes can help open up the third eye chakra as well. To get the most benefit out of this practice, try to focus on activities that involve being mindful and present such as meditation and yoga. Here are some helpful tips to consider:

- Take time for yourself each day to meditate or practice yoga.
- Make a conscious effort to be mindful and present in all of your activities throughout the day.
- Get into nature whenever possible, as this can help to ground you and awaken your third eye chakra.

Asanas/Yoga Poses

When finding the right poses for opening up the third eye chakra, focus on calming and uplifting postures. Forward folds such as seated forward bend and child's pose can release any tension from the head area connected to the third eye chakra. Inversions such as a supported shoulder stand and legs up the wall can balance this area by providing a sense of comfort and peace. Finally, supine poses, such as in transcendental meditation and *nadi shodhan pranayama,* can purify and open the third eye chakra.

Child's pose.
https://pixabay.com/es/photos/yoga-childs-pose-asana-2959214/

Awakening the Crown Chakra

Activating the crown chakra can be the catalyst for a life-altering experience of personal growth and transformation. Through this sacred process of introspection, our inner light can become brighter and more balanced. To awaken the crown, we must take a journey inwards. This includes examining our beliefs, becoming mindful of how we interact with others, and setting aside time for spiritual practice or meditation. As we do this work and let go of what no longer serves us, our awareness and understanding expand, which allows opportunities for personal growth. Our connection to divine energy is strengthened as we begin to open up the pathways within ourselves, allowing love, peace, and bliss to infuse every part of our being.

Diet Advice/Detox

Cleansing the crown chakra requires a mindful approach to diet. To spark vitality in this area, one should focus on eating light, fresh, organic foods rich in vitamins and minerals. Foods that contain phytonutrients (compounds produced by plants that provide health benefits to the body), such as berries, leafy greens, and cruciferous vegetables, are especially good for this area. Here are some helpful tips to consider:

- Eat a diet rich in dark leafy greens, berries, and cruciferous vegetables.
- Choose organic fruits and vegetables when possible.
- Limit your intake of processed foods and sugar.

Lifestyle Changes

In addition to diet, lifestyle plays an important role in activating the crown chakra. Regular exercise and relaxation are necessary to optimize the flow of energy between the chakras. Adding a simple stretching routine or yoga practice to your daily life can open up the pathways of energy and bring balance. Here are some helpful tips to consider:

- Take some time each day to practice simple stretching or yoga poses.
- Engage in activities that bring you joy, such as journaling or walking in nature.
- Make an effort to meditate or practice mindful breathing every day.

Asanas/Yoga Poses

Certain yoga postures specifically target the crown chakra. These postures help open up the energy pathways, allowing for the free energy flow between the mind and body. Headstand (Sirsasana) stimulates the crown chakra and encourages balance and clarity. Other postures that help awaken this area are the lotus pose (Padmasana), and corpse pose (Savasana). These poses help relax and open up the higher chakras providing a sense of oneness and peace.

Sirsasana pose.
https://www.pexels.com/photo/strong-woman-doing-sirsasana-posture-6454199/

As you work through this cleansing journey, remember to be gentle with yourself and stay open-minded. With consistency, patience, and perseverance, you can tap into the power of your energy and awaken the vibrant life force within you. By taking a mindful approach to diet, lifestyle, and yoga practices, we can awaken the crown chakra and experience a deeper level of spiritual connection. Through regular practice, we can begin to expand our consciousness and experience a more harmonious balance in our lives!

Chapter 4: Pranayama and Drishti: Focus and Breathe

Kundalini meditation and yoga are powerful tools that bridge our physical bodies to the energetic realm. Through intentional breathwork and posture, stagnant energy stored in the body is released while new, vibrant energy is called in. Practicing Kundalini meditation and yoga allows us to confront whatever riddles lie within ourselves and come out on a transformative journey of self-discovery. It opens up the opportunity to rediscover who we are at each level of consciousness, ultimately leading us back to our inner truth of oneness.

The ability to focus and breathe is fundamental to effective meditation.
https://unsplash.com/photos/rOn57CBgyMo

Kundalini yoga combines simple yet deeply embedded ancient practices with mantras used to anchor your divine creativity and power. This chapter focuses on two key components of Kundalini meditation and yoga, including Drishti (the eye gaze) and Pranayama (the regulation of the breath through certain techniques and exercises). It provides an understanding of both the eye gaze and the proper breathing techniques that can be used to support the journey of Kundalini meditation and yoga. By mastering the basics of these two components, you'll be able to take your Kundalini practice deeper and create the space for profound transformation.

Drishti - The Eye Gaze

Drishti is an integral concept in the practice of yoga. The directed gaze of awareness and purpose maintains focus on a particular point throughout a yoga practice. Practicing with Drishti helps us stay mindful and connected with our breath, our physical movements, and *ourselves*. By providing stability to the spine and calming the brain, this powerful tool takes us beyond the self-doubt and distractions that could obstruct us from deepening our connection with each pose. The concept of Drishti also teaches us to be conscious of what we gaze on in our lives outside yoga practice; as has been said, "we become what we behold." Drishti can help direct our inner eye in discovering what matters most to us in life.

A. What Is Drishti?

To be successful in Kundalini meditation and yoga, it is essential to understand what *Drishti* is. The word originates in Sanskrit and can be translated as "the eye gaze." It is the intentional and mindful direction of our sight. By using Drishti in yoga practice, we can keep our mind focused on a particular point, allowing us to connect with the breath and move through postures with intention. Iyengar Yoga, a type of modern yoga, defines the Drishti as "a gaze to bring awareness to its direction." While practicing Drishti, the eyes can be open or closed depending on the individual's preference.

B. Uses of Drishti in Kundalini Meditation and Yoga

Drishti stabilizes the mind and helps us attain mental clarity by allowing us to hold our concentration on one object for some time. We can further connect with our spiritual selves by focusing on one object during meditation. Using Drishti encourages conscious breathing to remain in each posture longer, increasing its benefits. Some kriyas (a specific set of exercises) require practitioners to gaze upward, downward, or outward towards horizons to align the body's energies and draw them inward toward the third eye center. Together, these practices create an environment that allows for more profound stillness and introspection.

1. Finding Focus

By focusing on energy and awareness, practitioners enter a meditative state and can begin to experience the full power of their practice. By concentrating on silent mantras or other stimuli, we can fully employ our physical and spiritual forces to reap all the benefits of Kundalini meditation and yoga. Although sometimes difficult for some newcomers to find such focus, when you have achieved it, it can lead to a deep understanding and appreciation of mediation practices.

2. Creating a Balanced Energy Flow

By gently focusing on different points in meditation or yoga postures, we can direct the energy that otherwise would be easily scattered throughout the body. This leads to greater internal awareness, as well as better mental clarity and emotional stability. Using Drishti during Kundalini meditation can create a deep meditative state, giving us access to the always-available inner resources of intuition and creativity. In summary, Drishti helps create a balanced energy flow that brings newfound vitality and healing into our lives.

3. Aligning Your Attention with Your Intentions

Using the visual power of Drishti to align your attention with your intentions is crucial in Kundalini meditation and yoga. When you focus on this practice, it gives you clarity and direction in life. With this type of focus and visualization, you gain deeper insight into yourself and more control over how you react to different experiences. As a result, your life can become more harmonious and balanced as your body posture changes and your energy aligns with your goals. These meditation techniques may be difficult at first, but once they become a regular part of your day, their influences will be transformative!

C. Specific Eye Focuses

Kundalini meditation and yoga are both ancient practices that involve specific eye focuses on unlocking a rich spiritual potential. In Kundalini meditation, practitioners concentrate their gaze on a single point while in a meditative practice designed to increase energy flow and inner awareness. Through this method, practitioners may experience a transcendent state of mental clarity, heightened intuition, and improved overall health and well-being.

Similarly, in yoga poses such as Padmasana or Mandukasana, practitioners are instructed to focus their eyes on an external object, typically one that connects them to the physical world. This practice, *trataka* (ir eye gazing), grounds the practitioner and fosters a deeper connection with nature. This simple yet profound practice allows yogis to deepen their concentration and obtain something greater than physical strength, a connection with divine understanding and peace within oneself. Through these specific eye focuses within Kundalini meditation and yoga, practitioners can access vast inner resources they never knew they had.

1. Brow Point

Developing your focus at the point between your brows leads to increased clarity of insight and intuition, which can then be used to manifest change and transformation in life. Learn how to practice the fine art of honing this mental acuity through pranayama or breath exercises, such as kriyas, chanting, and visualization. You'll find that when you train yourself to become aware of the brow point during your Kundalini meditations and yoga classes, you'll access a deeper level of stillness within, connecting you with a reservoir of inner strength and power.

2. Tip of the Nose

As Kundalini practitioners learn more about meditating, they access even deeper levels of consciousness by focusing their attention on the tip of the nose. Not only does this action increase sensory acuity and spatial awareness, but deriving from ancient yogic teachings, this technique improves how people respond to external stimuli and manage stress better. Regardless of your experience level or background in Yoga, learning how to focus your energy on the tip of your nose can bring great mental clarity, an essential piece for any successful Kundalini practice.

3. Chin

The practice of yoga and Kundalini meditation involves the specific use of eye focus for profound spiritual awakening. Focusing on the chin specifically, known as Chin Dharana, is a way to bring awareness to the third eye area that rests in the middle of the forehead, allowing connection with a higher level of consciousness. Though different techniques are required to activate this energy, a common practice among yogis is gazing between the eyebrows, corresponding with a rhythmical focus at the chin. This technique prepares one's body and mind for entering deep meditative states and encourages intensely powerful realizations that are an essential part of Kundalini yoga, making Chin Dharana an extremely powerful and valuable meditation technique.

4. Crown Chakra

The crown chakra, or Sahasrara, is the seventh major chakra in the body and governs wisdom, understanding, enlightenment, and connection to our inner divine self. Focusing your gaze on this chakra can help close the gap between the physical and spiritual realms. Focusing your eyes on a candle flame, an image of divinity, or even your thumb can ground you while providing an avenue to explore these higher realms. Whether you practice Kundalini meditation or yoga regularly or just when relaxing, these eye focuses can be beneficial tools for ultimate relaxation and awareness of your divine energy.

5. 1/10th Open

To tap into the Kundalini energy, practitioners of Kundalini meditation and Yoga use an eye-focus technique known as "1/10th Open," in which they keep their eyelids slightly open while mantras, visual images, or awareness to sensations of breath or an aspect of the physical body is present. This is a way to create a balance between being grounded in reality and creating mental space for concentrating the mind and connecting energetically to expand vision and creativity. 1/10th Open focuses on focusing attention while grounding the senses in physical reality through regular breathing techniques, eventually leading practitioners to newfound clarity, insight, and understanding.

Pranayama (The Proper Breathing)

Pranayama, or proper breathing, is integral to many types of yoga practice. This technique is used to regulate and control breath, improving both physical and mental health. Through this practice, one can increase their lung capacity, raise energy levels and create a sense of calmness. Proper breathing also improves our connection with the Universe and its inexhaustible energy source. With regular practice and dedication, a yogi can reach higher states of concentration through Pranayama and ultimately deepen their connection with the cosmos. Even beginners can start to see some benefits in just a few weeks if they stay consistent in their efforts.

A. What Is Pranayama?

Originating in India and formed from two Sanskrit words, Pranayama is an ancient practice associated with yoga. The two words combined to form Pranayama are "*Prana,*" meaning life force or breath, and "*Ayama,*" meaning control. Pranayama is a yogic technique that involves controlling and regulating the breath to improve one's physical health, mental clarity, and overall well-being. It involves breathing exercises to create a balance between the physical body and the mind.

B. Pranayama's Importance in Kundalini Awakening

Pranayama is a powerful tool for spiritual advancement and Kundalini awakening. By controlling the breath, one can create new energy pathways that unlock dormant energies within the body, allowing them to rise to bring greater consciousness and spiritual growth. Pranayama is also an effective way to reduce physical and mental tension so that meditation flows more easily. When combined with visualization practices, Ppranayama can open up new avenues of awakening the Kundalini force that lies dormant within everyone. This way, we can build stronger connections between our bodies, minds, and souls to get greater clarity and insight into truth and reality.

1. Connecting to Your Core

In Kundalini Awakening, Pranayama breathwork plays an essential role. Connecting you to your core and establishing a strong link between your spiritual and physical self, Pranayama is the first step in awakening the dormant energy within. Through conscious breathing exercises and cleansing of your mind and body, you begin to experience greater clarity, deeper concentration, and a stronger purpose. Pranayama allows you to tap into new depths of self-awareness and transformation that ultimately profoundly impact your life's journey. As you take control of your respiration, a higher level of consciousness and a renewed connection with yourself and the divine energy around you can be attained.

2. Increasing Awareness and Focus

The ancient practice of Pranayama is a cornerstone connection between mind and body. It increases one's awareness and focus. This practice can positively affect physical health and awaken the dormant energies in the chakras known as Kundalini. Pranayama enlightens the breath while deepening awareness of one's inner self. Through Pranayama, practitioners can learn how to be aware of their thoughts and feelings, which leads to healing and potential spiritual awakening.

Regular practice brings clarity to the body-mind connection, encouraging further exploration of meditation techniques and enabling people to channel their human potential for personal transformation and growth.

3. Energizing Your Meditation

Pranayama works at a cellular level to release toxins and can be used to tap into unlimited reserves of energy that permeate our meditation practice and aid in the awakening process. During a Pranayama session, we can eliminate blockages in our energetic body, allowing vital energy forces like chi and kundalini to flow freely and stir up spiritual progress by activating such things as chakras and karmic seed impressions. Meditators can reduce stress levels by developing greater control over their breath and mastering pranayama techniques while expanding their receptive abilities, leading to deeper states of meditation with higher spiritual payoffs.

C. Kundalini Breathing Exercises

Kundalini breathing exercises are a powerful tool for achieving peace and clarity within. These exercises have been used in spiritual practice for centuries to balance inner energies and cultivate good health, mental strength, and emotional resilience. They involve regulated breathing techniques that combine breath control with movement, postures, and meditation. By focusing on the breath, you can become aware of your inner emotions, leading to increased self-awareness and self-trust. Through systematic kundalini breathing exercises, practitioners feel more connected to their spiritual cores and more capable of cultivating positive states of mind.

1. Alternate Nostril Breathing

Alternate Nostril Breathing, also known as Nadi Shodhana Pranayama, is a potent Kundalini breathing exercise that works to balance the energies of the body and calm the mind by completing single full breaths through alternating nostrils. By controlling your inhalation and exhalation speed, you can bring your body into a state of greater balance. During this exercise, your breath creates a sound as it proceeds from one side and then back again, promoting relaxation. The process oxygenates all body parts, bringing clarity to our minds and increasing focus and concentration while reducing stress levels.

Steps:
1. Begin by sitting comfortably with your spine erect and eyes closed.
2. Place your left hand on your knee in a comfortable and relaxed position.
3. Place your right thumb over your right nostril and your ring finger over the left nostril.
4. Inhale deeply and slowly through your right nostril, then close it with your thumb.
5. Release your ring finger, and exhale slowly through your left nostril.
6. Remain in this position for a few moments, keeping your eyes closed.
7. Inhale deeply and slowly through your left nostril, then close it with your ring finger.
8. Release your thumb, and exhale slowly through your right nostril.
9. Remain in this position for a few moments, keeping your eyes closed.
10. Repeat this cycle for up to ten minutes and then stop, taking a few moments to relax in the stillness of your practice.

2. Breath of Fire

Breath of Fire is one of the most powerful breathing techniques to reduce physical and mental stress. It circulates your energy, cleanses your organs, and encourages increased prana (life force). This practice requires a smooth rhythmical pattern of conscious breathwork that alternates between equal lengths of inhalation and exhalation. Regularly doing these exercises can make you more relaxed, patient, and focused. Not only does this breathing technique provide physical wellness benefits such as reduced anxiety, but it also clears mental blockages that can keep us stuck in patterns of behavior and thought that limit us.

Steps:
1. Start in a comfortable seated position.
2. Place one hand on your lower abdomen and the other on your chest.

3. Begin rapid, shallow breathing through the nose with equal-length inhalations and exhalations.
4. Focus on your breath, allowing it to flow continuously while keeping a steady rhythm.
5. Feel the breath rise and fall in your abdomen and chest, respectively.
6. Continue for up to two minutes and then stop, taking a few moments to relax in the stillness of your practice.

3. Ujjayi Pranayama

Ujjayi pranayama is an ancient practice of mindful breathing originating in the tradition of Kundalini yoga. It promotes mental clarity, calmness, and inner balance. The basic technique involves inhaling slowly and deeply through the nose while slightly constricting the throat muscles, creating a soft "ocean wave" sound known as Ujjayi breath. This type of breathing fosters relaxation and quiets the mind and body by bringing awareness to the present moment. Practicing Ujjayi pranayama reduces stress, opens the body's energy centers, and activates higher states of consciousness. It provides numerous physical, emotional, and spiritual benefits for both beginners and experienced practitioners.

Steps:

1. Begin by sitting comfortably with your spine erect and eyes closed.
2. Take a few moments to relax, focusing on the natural breath.
3. Begin to inhale and exhale through the nose, taking deep breaths that expand the lungs as you inhale and contract them as you exhale.
4. Focus on the sound of your breath as it passes through the throat and notice how this creates a soft "ocean wave" type of sound.
5. Continue for up to 5-10 minutes, then release and relax in the stillness of your practice.

4. Long, Deep Breathing

Long, deep breathing exercises can be amazingly physically, mentally, and spiritually beneficial. Kundalini breathing is among the most popular of these exercises, combining aspects of traditional Eastern yogic practices with a more modern Westernized focus on energy centers and chakras. On a physiological level, Kundalini breathing relaxes muscles and organs in the body while stimulating neural cortex activity and clearing any potential blockages. On an emotional level, it promotes feelings of peace, confidence, and joy. Likewise, many practitioners find that regular practice offers deeper spiritual insights and access to higher levels of consciousness.

Steps:
1. Begin in a comfortable seated position. Close your eyes and take a few moments to relax, focusing on the natural breath.
2. Inhale deeply and slowly through the nose, directing the breath to fill your lungs from bottom to top.
3. When you reach the fullest inhalation possible, pause and hold your breath for a few seconds.
4. Exhale slowly and deeply through the nose, releasing as much air as possible.
5. Repeat the cycle for up to 10 minutes, then release and relax in the stillness of your practice.

Drishti and pranayama can be used together or separately as part of your kundalini practice. These powerful techniques enhance relaxation, clear mental blockages, and promote higher states of consciousness. When practiced regularly, they can offer tremendous physical, emotional, and spiritual benefits that are well worth the effort. This chapter has provided a brief overview of these two techniques and the steps involved in practicing them. We hope this introduction helps inspire your exploration of Kundalini meditations and Pranayama breathing exercises. Happy awakening!

Chapter 5: Unlocking Energy with Mudras and Mantras

Mudras and mantras are two spiritual practices that yogis have used for centuries. Mudras involve forming special hand gestures to help cultivate inner peace and stimulate the Kundalini energy. Mantras are sacred words, phrases, or syllables that can be chanted or repeated silently in meditation to manifest positive change or amplify energy flow. When combined, mudras and mantras can open up the energy pathways throughout the body, allowing for deeper healing and transformation. They are powerful tools for releasing trapped emotions and restoring vibrant health, balance, and well-being.

Mudras and mantras help center your balance and focus.
https://unsplash.com/photos/n8L1VYaypcw

This chapter will cover the role of mudras and mantras in Kundalini awakening and yoga. It will also discuss their general benefits as well as provide a list of the most useful and potent mudras and mantras for practicing Kundalini yoga. The specific meanings and chakra activations of the Kundalini mantras will also be discussed. While mudras and mantras are deeply intertwined, this chapter will discuss them separately to better understand the practices. By the end of this chapter, you'll have a much deeper understanding of mudras and mantras and how to use them to awaken your Kundalini energy.

Mudras

Mudras are a type of hand gesture commonly seen in ancient Indian art, such as statues and paintings. Mudras tap into the power of prana, or life energy, and have specific meanings that are thought to bring about physical health and spiritual insight. For example, the Abhaya Mudra conveys protection, courage, and blessings from the divine, Gyan Mudra aids in balance and enlightenment, Dharmachakra Mudra is an invocation for truth, and the Varada Mudra symbolizes charity. Surya Mudra is believed to improve metabolism, Añjali Mudra awakens compassion and humility, and Dhyana Mudra encourages meditation and connection. Practicing these mudras can be a powerful healing tool on all levels.

A. The Role and Concept of Mudras

Mudras represent several sacred meanings ranging from simple to complex and vary across cultures and practices. Like Hinduism's Namaskara mudra of greeting and respect for the teachings of yoga, these ritualistic symbols are infused with an inner power that helps invoke strong emotions associated with different spiritual concepts. Mudras offer a powerful path for achieving a personal connection to higher consciousness and understanding if used accurately and respectfully. Practitioners often use these meaningful postures in meditation or prayer to access greater insight or reflect on specific feelings toward inner truth or enlightenment.

B. Benefits of Mudras

Kundalini Yoga offers an array of benefits, from increased physical strength and stability to enhanced spiritual and emotional well-being. One of its unique aspects is the mudras that draw upon the body's energy, enabling practitioners to gain even more from their practice.

These hand gestures can be used for various purposes, such as helping to control breath, balancing the chakras, and calming the mind. Used correctly, mudras can help Kundalini yoga practitioners reach a deep connection with themselves that is difficult to achieve through other forms of yoga or meditation. A consistent practice of using mudras in Kundalini yoga sessions creates a strong link between the mind and body while allowing a deeper understanding and acceptance of one's self.

1. Physical Benefits

One of the first steps a yogi will learn in Kundalini yoga is a set of mudras or hand positions. Each mudra has a particular meaning associated with it. But beyond the symbolism, one area in which Kundalini has excelled is unlocking specific bodily benefits through harnessing energy and movement, largely due to these helpful mudras. Just as our hands can be quite expressive when we're communicating verbally, they can also demonstrate healing power via these subtle shifts while practicing Kundalini yoga. By unlocking each chakra system, with different mudras representing each region within us, we understand which areas require more attention than others. This imaginative exploration increases circulation to promote healthier muscles and joints throughout the body while developing physical and emotional strength grounded in self-exploration!

2. Mental Benefits

One of the main ways to achieve self-awareness and create balance is by using mudras. Mudras reduce stress and anxiety, increase focus, boost creativity, and improve clarity in thinking. By bringing attention to the hands and nurturing mindfulness, mudras can bring us into a more grounded and present state of being. Furthermore, combining them with breath work can induce a meditative state that further opens us up to our inner wisdom. So, it's easy to see that, practiced regularly, mudras can significantly benefit our mental health.

3. Spiritual Benefits

One integral part of using mudras in Kundalini yoga is to increase spiritual energy throughout the body. Mudras redirect subtle energy within the body, clearing blockages and creating balance and harmony. Each mudra has spiritual benefits, allowing us to open our hearts and minds, helping us to enter a deep meditative state, commune with spirituality, and potentially bring about a heightened awareness as we move closer to enlightenment. Those who regularly practice Kundalini yoga and its accompanying mudras can experience profound spiritual growth as they deepen their physical and mental well-being.

C. Useful and Potent Mudras for Kundalini Yoga

Yoni Mudra, Bhairavi Mudra, and Shunya Mudra are three useful and potent mudras for activating Kundalini energies. Yoni Mudra symbolizes starting from the seed of creation and is meant to connect us with our spiritual essence. Bhairavi Mudra stimulates intuition, courage, enthusiasm, and creativity. It strengthens inner wisdom. On the other hand, Shunya Mudra focuses on stillness and clarity within ourselves. Several mudras can help us become more mindful of our breath, relaxation, centering, and concentration, all components of Kundalini yoga.

1. Kundalini Mudra

The powerful Kundalini Mudra opens the chakras in the body, allowing them to be filled with energy, and recognizes imbalances that need correcting. The fingers cover different points throughout the body, encouraging a tranquil yet alert flow of energy as if simultaneously charging all parts of your body. When using these mudras, you may notice a heightened sense of balance, clarity, and harmony that strengthens with each repetition or skillful movement. With consistent practice, the full benefits of Kundalini Mudras can truly be experienced!

2. Uddiyan Bandha

Uddiyan Bandha is a powerful mudra and yoga technique rooted in traditional Kundalini yoga. Uddiyan Bandha translates to flying or upward lock, which refers to the visceral lifts of the muscles in the stomach area that this mudra requires. It flushes stale energies and awakens creativity and positive energy. Practicing Uddiyan Bandha challenges you to reawaken your life force. It eliminates fatigue, anxiety, depression, and other negative emotions while promoting physical strength, agility, and resilience. It is an effective form of relaxation, encouraging deep breathing, which can help clear the mind and body of built-up stress. People who practice Uddiyan Bandha regularly have also reported benefits such as improved digestion and toned abdominal muscles. It can be integrated into any practice involving yoga flow or postures with ample rest time between exercises for greater mental and physical benefits.

3. Mahamudra

Mahamudra, developed by Yogi Bhajan and practiced worldwide, helps practitioners relax and become grounded during meditation. It is a useful way to access your body and soul's energy, allowing you to open up pathways that are closed off from everyday life. When practicing Mahamudra regularly, one can find clarity and an overall sense of well-being within. Anyone who practices this mudra will experience profound shifts in their mental, physical, and spiritual health. The benefits of this mudra include a deeper connection with one's true potential, inner peace, and enhanced intuition. With consistent effort, you can reach powerful energetic states essential for healing on all levels. Given such magical properties, it is clear why Mahamudra has become so popular amongst those practicing Kundalini yoga today.

4. Apana Mudra

The Apana Mudra is another extremely beneficial and potent mudra pose for practicing Kundalini yoga. It is beneficial because it releases any stagnant energy in the body and promotes energy circulation from the lower abdomen toward the feet. With this pose, practitioners will get an increased awareness and grounding in their bodies and a greater connection between body and mind. Practicing this mudra regularly will enhance strength and flexibility, energize organs, purify the blood, improve digestion, balance hormones, and increase fertility. This balanced practice provides a feeling of empowering stability while stimulating creativity and boosting joy.

5. Gyana Mudra

The Gyana Mudra, also known as the Gyan Mudra or Jnana Mudra, is a crucial part of Kundalini yoga. It involves stretching your fingers so that your thumb and first two fingers form a circle, with the remaining fingers curling towards the palm. Also known as the "seal of knowledge," this potent mudra is believed to awaken inner wisdom and unlock intellectual power. Practitioners of Kundalini yoga use this mudra to enter a deep meditative state, resulting in increased concentration, clarity of thought, and higher states of consciousness. In addition to its spiritual benefits, Gyana Mudra reduces stress and induces relaxation, as well as relieves carpal tunnel-like issues caused by repetitive motions experienced by people doing typing or repetitive heavy work. In summary, Gyana Mudra is certainly a useful practice for those interested in advancing their physical well-being and spiritual awareness.

Mantras

Mantras are an ancient form of chanting used to connect with a higher power since the beginning of time. Each mantra has its individual significance and meaning, which can focus you on universal energy and help you reach a blissful meditation state. Mantras have no limits in terms of purpose and use, as they can be chanted to enter into the space of inner peace, channel the universe's energy, strengthen faith and willpower, or learn more about oneself. Regardless of the goal you try to achieve through your mantra practice, you're guaranteed to move towards a meaningful life filled with tranquility and harmony.

A. Prayers for Kundalini

Prayers for Kundalini are becoming increasingly popular for spiritual healing and growth. When used with prayer, the Kundalini energy is enhanced and can produce increased mental acuity, improved physical health, deeper spiritual connection, and more profound emotional clarity. Regular practice can open up doorways to new forms of self-awareness and a greater understanding of life's mysteries. Kundalini prayers have been used for centuries as a powerful tool in one's spiritual journey and can bring about both personal inner peace and worldly balance.

1. Kirtan Sohila

Kirtan Sohila is an ancient Sikh prayer for Kundalini energy and awakening of the soul. It is recited daily by Sikhs before going to bed. Kirtan Sohila gently washes away any worries and anxieties, bringing in a state of deep relaxation, peace, and calmness. Its divine words travel through the layers of the physical body and connect us directly to our true divine self, pure consciousness beyond time, space, and formlessness. One experiences a sense of union with the Universal Consciousness in its meditative chant. This blessing experience can bring well-being to one's life on all levels, physically, emotionally, mentally, spiritually, and transcendentally.

2. Guru Ram Das Prayer

Guru Ram Das is revered as the fourth Sikh Guru and chief of five beloved Gurus. His legacy connects us to an ancient devotional tradition of transformational Kundalini meditation. Through his inspiring words, he speaks to us still, particularly through the timeless prayer for Kundalini. This powerful mantra calls upon divine intervention to unlock the flow of spiritual energy within, expressing a desire to know freedom and find love in our hearts and souls. The results are profound, awakening the dormant spirit within, calming depression and fear, and enabling each individual to experience true fulfillment in life.

3. Vishnu Sahasranam

Vishnu Sahasranam, a prayer dedicated to Lord Vishnu, is believed to be powerful enough to awaken your dormant Kundalini energy. The prayer can help you tap into your inner strength and connects you with the divine force within you. By chanting it regularly, one can attain inner peace and clarity, as well as strengthen your connection with the divine source. Vishnu Sahasranam comprises 1000 different names of Lord Vishnu, each of which acts as a spiritual growth tool. Experienced Yogis suggest that this kind of practice gives positive results if practiced with sincerity, dedication, and attention. Doing so allows you to manifest your desires and appreciate life from a larger perspective.

B. Kundalini Mantras

Kundalini mantras are powerful chants believed to give practitioners an added spiritual boost when practiced regularly. These mantras also aim to open up the energy at the base of the spine, where the dormant Serpent Power lies. Although they are used as part of a particular style of yoga, their effect can be called on by anyone who has committed them to memory and meditated on their meaning. Some people also find that chanting these mantras in certain combinations and with certain sounds can benefit their physical, mental, and spiritual well-being. With many Kundalini mantras available, each practitioner can find one or several that resonate deeply with them and use them as part of their path to self-discovery.

1. Adi Mantra

Om Namo Guru Dev Namo

Meaning: "I bow to the Divine within myself, my guru."

Adi Mantra is used in meditation and yoga to activate divine energies, bringing us closer to the Divine. Through daily repetition of the Adi Mantra, its spiritual power works to balance our inner chakras, helping us tap into the infinite consciousness and spiritual strength that already exists within ourselves. Each cycle of this mantra brings energetic healing, allowing you to feel more connected and open to spiritual evolution. "Adi" translates to primordial nature in many cultures worldwide, reflecting the powerhouse of the healing potential that can be unlocked by activating the chakras through the Adi Mantra. As we journey on this path towards enlightenment and soul expansion, the regular practice of chanting the Adi Mantra allows us to relax more completely and deepen our spiritual understanding of ourselves and our relationships with others.

2. Mangala Charn Mantra

Aad Guray Nameh, Jugad Guray Nameh, Sat Guray Nameh, Siri Guru Devay Nameh

Meaning: "I bow to the primal guru, I bow to the wisdom throughout the ages, I bow to the true guru, I bow to great divine wisdom."

Mangala Charn Mantra is an ancient and powerful Kundalini mantra from the Upanishads that invoke Lord Shiva and Goddess Parvati to bring forth divine energy. The word "Mangala" means "auspicious," and it can invigorate the seven chakras for spiritual growth. This mantra brings greater peace, joy, clarity of purpose, and satisfaction by opening the heart to love and compassion. It can also assist in healing physical, emotional, psychological, and spiritual issues. Additionally, this mantra activates each chakra, connecting each area of one's life to that particular chakra, such as creativity or relationships, to move closer toward well-being. Therefore, chanting Mangala Charn Mantra is a powerful practice for true transformation.

3. Mul Mantra

Ek Onkar Sat Nam Karta Purakh Nirbhau Nirvair Akal Murat Ajuni Saibhang Gur Prasad

Meaning: "There is one Creator of all, truth is its name, doer of everything, fearless and without enmity, beyond time, beyond form and self-illuminated. May this be granted to us by Guru's Grace."

The *Mul Mantra*, or "root mantra,"' is an ancient Hindu one that has provided immense power and spiritual healing to seekers worldwide for centuries. Its poetic composition opens the gateway to a profound spiritual understanding while awakening our Kundalini Shakti. Translated from ancient Sanskrit, one of the meanings behind the Mul Mantra is "I open myself up to experience the Divine within." Its resonance activates the root chakra, is essential for good health and well-being, and releases any blockages along our spine to allow us to move through life with creativity and full presence. Participating in this ancient practice of gaining access to inner divinity and unlocking one's infinite potential is a special experience that can be cherished forever.

4. Shri Gayatri Mantra

Om Bhur Bhuva Swaha, Tat Savitur Varenyam, Bhargo Devasaya Dheemahi, Dhiyo Yo Nah Prachodayat

Meaning: "We meditate on the divine light of Savitur; may it inspire and illumine our minds and hearts."

Shri Gayatri Mantra is an ancient chant said to activate the third eye or Ajna Chakra. It has become a cornerstone in Kundalini yoga and meditation as it invokes universal wisdom and guides spiritual awakening within a practitioner. The mantra's deepening effects come from its many layers of meaning and resonance. Humbling, inspiring, and deeply powerful, this invocation brings many profound benefits, including mental clarity, improved sleep, increased intuition, enhanced concentration, and greater insight into the true nature of conscious awareness. With regular practice and other meditative lifestyle measures like diet and breathing exercises, practitioners can expect to experience profound transformation through their work with Shri Gayatri Mantra.

5. Akal Ustat

Waho Akal Ki Ustat, Jo Tum Akhand Path Kare

Meaning: "Hail to the Praise of the Eternal One, He who recites the Eternal Word."

Akal Ustat is a potent mantra from the Sikh tradition and has been used for centuries to bring about deep spiritual healing. It was designed to call upon the divine energy of the universe, and its resonance is said to activate all seven chakras. This mantra invokes the divine teacher to uplift our consciousness, fill us with courage, and help us find inspiration in difficult times. Akal Ustat is believed to purify the karmic field and all of our subtle bodies and is an incredibly powerful tool for Kundalini yoga practitioners. When chanted out loud, Akal Ustat can bring about deep relaxation and inner peace while also calming the mind and aiding in meditation practice. As such, it is a wonderful resource for your Kundalini yoga practice.

The power of mantras and mudras is undeniable. While both have been used for centuries to bring about personal transformation, they are only fully realized when used in conjunction with regular Kundalini yoga and meditation practice. With a deeper understanding of the energetics behind each mudra and mantra, practitioners can gain insight into the unique gifts and capabilities of each, allowing them to more fully realize the potential within their practice. As one begins to explore the vast potential of Kundalini yoga and meditation, these mudras and mantras can be used as powerful tools to bring about transformation and spiritual awakening!

Chapter 6: How to Do Kundalini Meditation

Kundalini meditation is a powerful way to access spiritual power and energy within yourself. With practice and dedication, one can awaken the Kundalini energy, known as the "serpent power," which exists at the base of the spine. This powerful energy replaces negative thoughts and creates an immense sense of joy and spiritual balance when accessed. By combining ancient yoga techniques with relaxing breathwork and visualization, Kundalini meditation uncovers our ultimate potential, both spiritually and mentally. Through this yogic practice, we search deeply into our souls for healing, strength, courage, self-awareness, and inner peace.

Kundalini meditation allows us to clear our minds, relax our bodies, quieten inner chatter, connect with our spirit guides, and come closer to whichever higher power we believe in. This chapter will explain what Kundalini meditation is and its benefits, the step-by-step instructions on practicing it, and provide some tips on how to enhance it. Ultimately, with consistency and dedication, Kundalini meditation can help to create a better connection to the divine and yourself.

What Is Kundalini Meditation?

Kundalini meditation is revolutionizing the way people approach spirituality and self-development. Through a combination of deep breathing techniques, yoga postures, mantras, and visualizations,

Kundalini meditation brings a spiritual element to a physical practice. Primarily focusing on channeling energy that rises from the base of the spine up through the body, these meditations bring mental and physical balance. With so many different combinations available, Kundalini meditation can be tailored to fit anyone's needs. Whether someone wants to focus on internal dialogue or work on manifesting desired outcomes in their life, there is a Kundalini meditation for each stage of personal transformation.

Benefits of Kundalini Meditation

Kundalini meditation helps practitioners to access the universal energy within themselves and bring the body, mind, and spirit into alignment. Many followers who practice it find that it brings many benefits, such as improved physical and mental health, greater spiritual development, enhanced creativity and intuition, improved clarity of thought, and better concentration and focus. Furthermore, as it encourages a more centered lifestyle, practitioners of Kundalini often report feeling more connected to themselves and the wider world. In essence, Kundalini meditation is a path toward understanding one's true purpose in life.

1. Increase Creativity

This powerful practice promotes creativity, agility of the mind, and emotional stability. It unlocks suppressed creative energy and aids in tapping into one's creative potential. Through regular Kundalini meditation, you'll find that you have increased focus and clarity of thought, can create inspirational ideas, and foster a positive emotional state. Kundalini meditation also creates the perfect ambiance for self-reflection and spiritual growth, which helps us connect with our intuition and access the unconscious part of ourselves. As a result, we can discern what truly inspires us, expand upon our current thought processes, and become more original in our concept creation. Ultimately, Kundalini Meditation helps open the pathway towards finding multiple ways of creativity that reflect our selves.

2. Balancing the Nervous System

Kundalini meditation is gaining traction as a technique to naturally balance the nervous system. Through its emphasis on patience, focus, and understanding, Kundalini meditation creates an equilibrium between mind and body. When practiced regularly, this technique can help individuals cultivate inner peace and better manage their emotions. It can also serve to lower stress levels as well as reduce anxiety. As a result of these effects, practitioners will often face life's obstacles with ease by better managing both physical and mental health.

3. Enhancing Intuition

Through the growth and expansion that this inner spiritual power brings, practitioners can dramatically enhance their intuition. Those who use Kundalini meditation have improved cognitive abilities and a greater sense of insight. This results in better decision-making processes, more creative problem-solving skills, and heightened awareness of environments. Thus, it gives users a more holistic understanding of their existence and reality, helping them gain an otherworldly perspective on life's matters. By strengthening intuition, we can clearly understand our purpose in life and be guided towards becoming contented individuals.

4. Improves Mental Clarity

Meditating through Kundalini is a forceful method of improving mental clarity. While many studies have proven the benefits of meditation, it is especially powerful when combined with moving postures and breathing exercises, which start to activate and balance energetic pathways in the body. Practicing Kundalini meditation frees any mental blocks formed from stress and anxiety, giving you a greater perspective and ability better solve tough problems. Regular practice helps foster clarity, creativity, and concentration skills, which can improve decision-making capabilities for daily life, whether on a personal or professional level.

5. Stimulates Better Sleep

Practicing Kundalini meditation can be a great way to relax and recharge to get a better night's sleep. When you meditate, you breathe deeply, which relaxes your body and slows down the heart rate. This can help our brains transition more quickly from the day's stress into a restful sleep state. In addition, Kundalini meditation enables us to explore our emotions and process them healthily, leaving us calm and encouraging better sleep. Releasing built-up tension helps us fall asleep faster, stay asleep longer, and wake up feeling energized. These benefits make it clear that taking time out of your day for a Kundalini meditation session can be essential for getting a better night's sleep.

6. Reduces Stress and Anxiety

This ancient form of Indian meditation brings the ability to reduce stress and anxiety through breathwork, chanting mantras, movements, and visualization to connect deeply with oneself. Kundalini meditation creates feelings of relaxation by releasing endorphins that reduce cortisol levels and decrease anxiety. The movement component encourages people to release any negative emotions they're holding onto while increasing their self-awareness. Kundalini meditation not only aids in reducing stress but reduces physical symptoms such as headaches and back pain. This meditation helps people stay more present in the moment while being mindful of their thoughts and feelings, enabling them to live life with greater fulfillment, peace, and satisfaction.

7. Clears the Subconscious Mind

Kundalini meditation has been practiced for thousands of years and is said to be the work of the gods, providing a path to enlightening the minds of mere mortals. It combines intention, sound, and breath as a discipline to clear the subconscious mind. Long-term practitioners swear that Kundalini meditation opens them up to possibilities not accessible before, from increased creativity and mental clarity to greater self-confidence. Consequently, they tap into their deepest meditative space at will, resulting in profound insights and personal breakthroughs that can revolutionize their lives. Ultimately, clearing our subconscious through Kundalini meditation enables us to unveil the blueprint of ourselves with newfound clarity and purpose.

8. Fosters Self-Awareness

Over time, this meditative practice also fosters self-awareness. People who practice it can observe the changes occurring within their inner consciousness. This leads to a greater understanding of one's self, which can be a wonderful journey of growth and understanding. As an individual becomes increasingly aware of their inner workings and gains insight into their behavior and its effects on the world around them, they can make decisions that improve both their life and the lives of those they share it with. Therefore, Kundalini meditation is truly a valuable gift by promoting self-awareness and the overall health of body and mind.

9. Regulates Emotions

Practicing Kundalini can help one better understand oneself, that is, a better understanding of our physical sensations and emotions. With this knowledge, it becomes easier to identify, understand and process negative feelings without letting them take control. The mental clarity achieved by Kundalini allows for a perspective that can help calm the mind and gain control over erratic thoughts or compulsions. It effectively cultivates patience, understanding, acceptance of oneself, and increased emotional stability, leading to better relationships. In other words, a regular Kundalini practice promotes mindfulness of feelings and intelligent responses that are beneficial for everyone involved.

10. Improved Overall Health

Regular meditation practice can improve physical, mental, and emotional well-being as the mind becomes calmer, stress levels lower, and self-confidence increases. People who have adopted it into their routine have reported having better cognitive functions and improved responses to inflammation-related diseases such as arthritis and lupus. Practicing Kundalini also releases energy from various parts of the brain, resulting in improved overall health. It enables a person to stay motivated and proactive while setting goals and working towards achieving them. Therefore, this form of meditation can help anyone to create an overall healthy lifestyle that promotes long-term wellness.

Step-by-Step Instructions for Kundalini Meditation

It is surprisingly simple to get started, but like most good things in life, it does require commitment and dedication to foster its full potential. By setting aside time each day for practice, you can enjoy the countless benefits of this ancient practice, from improved emotional clarity and enhanced self-awareness to heightened intuition and spiritual presence. A synthesizing of breath work, mantras, and postures with awareness toward inner wisdom creates an enriching experience that encourages holistic transformation both inwards and outwards. Here are the basic steps to get started:

1. Set the Intention

Setting an intention for your Kundalini meditation can help you focus on your goals and bring more clarity to your practice. Start by quieting your mind and taking a few deep breaths. Finally, take some time to self-reflect with an open heart and mind, to determine what you want to get out of the meditation. Determine how you want to grow from the experience and set clear intentions regarding what you aim for spiritually, mentally, emotionally, or physically. Be specific about why your intention matters for where you want to go in life. With a strong foundation in place and positive affirmations added to the mix, a

Kundalini meditation immersed with intention can reshape your mindset and alter your perspective. Through this powerful practice, experience a deeper connection between yourself and the cosmic realm.

2. Choose a Meditation Posture

When choosing a meditation posture, choose one that supports your body and allows you to be comfortable for an extended period. Traditionally, this is done in a seated position, such as on the floor, cushion, or chair. Suppose any physical limitations make it difficult for you to sit for long periods. In that case, there are lying postures used in Kundalini meditation as well. The most vital thing is to find the posture that allows your back and neck to be evenly supported so that your muscles don't tire out during the meditation. Whichever posture you choose will help set the foundation for peace and stillness while opening yourself up to Kundalini energy within your body.

3. Focus on Your Breath

Focusing on your breath while meditating with Kundalini techniques will reduce stress and psychological trauma while also connecting you with your spiritual or higher self effectively. When focusing on your breath during Kundalini meditation, be mindful of the depth and length of each inhalation and exhalation. This mindfulness allows practitioners to create a reflective space within themselves, giving them access to their truest potential by awakening their inner energies. With practice, any individual can profoundly connect with Kundalini energy through mindful breathing during Kundalini meditation.

4. Connect to the Divine

By connecting ourselves to the divine, we can go beyond our everyday thoughts and into a state of knowledge, understanding, and peace that can be difficult to find in our chaotic modern lives. We can access this special level of awareness through Kundalini meditation, chanting mantras, and focusing on certain body parts to create more balance in our energy flow. Once we connect with the divine, it gives us the courage to take on whatever challenge we may face and the capacity for great inner peace. Whether searching for a way to reduce anxiety or seek spiritual growth, connecting to the divine through Kundalini meditation will give you a strong foundation to begin your journey.

5. Do Not Force Meditation

Kundalini meditation should never be forced. Different people will experience this form of meditation in distinct and unique ways, so it's crucial to remain open-minded and not expect a particular outcome. As practitioners become more experienced with the technique, they are likely to further develop their skills and refine the meditation process as needed. It is essential to give your body and mind time to adjust during each session, as some forms of Kundalini can be very intense. Only practice with a teacher with experience and knowledge about such an intricate form of meditation. When done correctly, this meditation can become incredibly powerful and move energy through your chakras like no other.

6. Use Mantras and Mudras

Finding inner peace and balance can be challenging for many in today's hectic and often stressful world. Kundalini meditation can be an effective tool in helping us reach this tranquility. Using mantras and mudras will deepen one's experience and lead to profound transformation. Mantras are chanting sounds that help increase our awareness, while mudras involve specific hand gestures to focus the mind, aid concentration, and bring greater clarity. Combined with traditional yoga postures, they produce an even greater effect, encouraging the mind and body to open up more deeply and cultivate a serene atmosphere conducive to achieving lasting balance.

7. End Your Session with Gratitude

One way to ensure you make the most of Kundalini meditation is to end your session with gratitude. Consider what this unique experience has given you, perhaps a feeling of peace or insight about yourself, and be thankful for it. Allow gratitude to permeate your mind and body as you close off the meditation session, carrying positive energy into your daily life. The more you practice, the more consistent and powerful its effects can become. The key is to remain open and willing to experience something new each time you practice Kundalini meditation.

Tips for Enhancing Your Kundalini Meditation Experience

Uncovering an intensified sense of tranquility and awareness through a Kundalini meditation practice can be incredibly rewarding. With practice, anyone can use it to detach from worldly worries and gain insight into their innermost thoughts and emotions. Being open-minded and focused on the practice, not just during meditation sessions but through daily life, will be the most beneficial way to make progress with this form of meditation. Here are some tips to help you get the most out of your Kundalini meditation experience.

1. Create a Sacred Space

Creating a sacred space for Kundalini meditation is an excellent way to enhance your experience and get the most out of practice. This could involve bringing in elements and items such as incense, calming music, candles, yoga chairs or bolsters, essential oils, and more. Doing this in advance will help you relax into your Kundalini session, improving focus and attention while encouraging a deeper state of tranquility. Incorporating personal objects such as photos or totems can also be beneficial in helping to create a comfortable atmosphere that resonates with your spiritual needs. Ultimately, having this dedicated space that allows you to pause and reflect without distraction is key to cultivating a positive journey through Kundalini meditation.

2. Wear Comfortable Clothing

To get the most out of a deep, spiritual experience, wear comfortable and unrestricted clothing. Clothing should also provide some coverage if lying on the ground, as particular revealing postures may be called for during Kundalini meditation. Opting for loose, breathable fabrics such as organic cotton or hemp and layered pieces that can be easily added or removed are great choices when exploring Kundalini meditation. Making sure comfort comes first will allow meditators to stay focused on the many mental and spiritual benefits of this life-transforming experience.

3. Practice at the Same Time Every Day

Regular and consistent Kundalini practice is one of the most crucial aspects of enhancing your meditation experience. Practicing at the same time every day will give you structure, stability, and quality to your meditations. When your body learns the daily habit, it eventually enters into a trance-like state of meditation more easily and quickly. When practiced in a relaxed fashion at the same time each day, you build momentum for deeper concentration levels and an enhanced transformation through connection with spirit. Establishing a Kundalini practice as part of a daily routine helps promote emotional well-being for those seeking peace, healing, and joy.

4. Incorporate Essential Oils

Incorporating essential oils while practicing Kundalini meditation can be a lovely, serene way to enhance your experience. Essential oils have been used for centuries in spiritual and healing ceremonies, and their aromatic properties can influence your intention and mental focus. They can also open up the body's chakra centers which are key for unlocking Kundalini energy. Start by adding a few drops of essential oils such as Frankincense, Lavender, or Basil to a diffuser, or use them topically by applying them around the heart, throat, and lower brow areas with light massage strokes. Discover how essential oils can transport you into deeper states of meditation and expand your connection to the spiritual world.

5. Visualize a Goal

With the right visualizations and imagery, you can improve your experience. Having a clear picture of what you want to achieve through meditation can help you stay focused during practice and create deeper relaxation within yourself. By visualizing the outcome you want from your meditation journey, whether feeling calm, connected to nature, or released from stress, your mind will be even more attuned to the effects of breathing meditations, mantras, and other spiritual exercises. Acknowledging desired outcomes during a session can put you in control of your path toward realization. Anchor yourself to the goal so your journey is more successful with each practice.

6. Journal Reflections

Enhancing your Kundalini meditation experience can be difficult. However, journaling reflections on your meditation practice can help you to quantify and track improvements. Reflecting on the time spent in meditation allows you to better comprehend the sensations experienced and augment your understanding of what is occurring during the practice. It can act as a motivator to deepen and continue your practice and reveal where modifications may be required. Regular journaling allows one to connect with inner truths and unlock new spiritual realms that are otherwise inaccessible.

7. Practice Meditation in Nature

Many people don't realize that the environment in which you practice meditation has a lot to do with the positive effects they can experience. Kundalini meditation done in nature can be particularly enhanced because of the natural energy present in outdoor environments.

Practicing outside lets practitioners connect directly with their inner selves and benefit from Mother Nature's healing energy. Exposure to fresh air, sunshine, plants, and animals can also have many physiological benefits, including improved immune systems and reduced fatigue. So, for those looking to take their meditation practice up a notch, being at one with nature is worth considering.

Kundalini Meditation is an ancient practice that has the potential to bring about great transformation and healing in those who are willing to commit to its practice. Through regular practice, one can experience profound spiritual transformation and unlock your full potential. You can take your Kundalini meditation practice to the next level with simple tips, such as incorporating essential oils, visualizing a goal, journaling reflections, and practicing in nature. With consistent effort and dedication, anyone can experience the potential benefits of this powerful meditative practice.

Chapter 7: Arambha: A Root Awakening

As we progress along the serpent's path of spiritual awakening, we can observe the Kundalini energy rise to open and clear each of the many chakras that line our spines. This is an often compared process with much symbolism and strength embedded within it. The term "Kundalini" can also be translated to mean "the curl of the lock of hair of the beloved" and represents the creative power in all consciousness. A thorough understanding of this transformational journey is full of revelations that take us to deeper places within ourselves, bringing awareness to both new possibilities as well as ancient truths.

This chapter of the Kundalini Yoga Guide introduces and guides you through the first stage of Kundalini awakening, Arambha. Here, we will discuss what happens during this stage, which chakras are affected, how they can affect your life, and the untied knots. We will then present simple step-by-step instructions for a few kriyas and sequences that target the stimulation of this stage, as well as some balancing postures and pranayama practices to support this process. Finally, we will close with a few meditations to integrate this whole experience.

The First Stage of Kundalini Awakening

Arambha, or the first stage of the Kundalini awakening process, is a deeply emotional and transformative experience. This initial phase is miraculous, as it sets a life-altering introspective journey in motion. On an energetic level, it begins a purification process and re-adjustment of subtle energies within the body. During Arambha, a person may feel a penetrating heat come through their body as if their chi was being awakened from its dormant state. As this wave of energy builds, physical pain can be experienced as tensions are released from deep within our body. During this stage, it is essential to maintain balance and not overextend oneself beyond what is comfortable. The practice of self-love and non-attachment can often provide support for navigating through this profound journey to find joy in sacred metamorphosis.

A. What Happens during Arambha

Arambha is the first stage of the Kundalini awakening process and involves a process of profound transformation. The innermost energies lying dormant in an individual are woken due to increased spiritual activity. The power of this exchange releases energetic blockages within the body, allowing pure, unconditional love to lift one beyond limitations into higher states of consciousness. Several phenomena often occur during Arambha, such as intuitive knowledge or altered states of mental, emotional, and physical awareness. In some cases, even psychic abilities such as clairvoyance or healing powers can come into play. Arambha is an incredibly transformative experience that allows one to journey sublimely toward cosmic consciousness.

B. Chakras Affected and Their Effects

Our chakras are affected during Arambha (the first stage of Kundalini awakening). Each of the seven main chakras is activated, energized, and balanced as we progress on this spiritual journey. Our root chakra is connected to a sense of security and being grounded. As it heals and opens, we begin to feel more secure within ourselves and connect more deeply with the physical world around us. Our sacral chakra deals with our emotional intelligence, sensuality, and creativity and helps us become aware of our life's purpose. Healing this chakra increases intuition and caring towards self and others while lessening any attachments that may have held us back from achieving our true potential.

All the chakras are influenced during Arambha.
https://commons.wikimedia.org/wiki/File:Yoga_all_chakras_and_chakraserpent.png

Our solar plexus holds much of our motivations, determination, power, influence over others, and even personal identity. Mental clarity increases when energy starts flowing here again, allowing for strong trust in one's decisions. This can be a powerful motivator for doing things we want to do or that our soul craves for itself in terms of increasing spirituality. All in all, these aroused energies work together to holistically rejuvenate each aspect of day-to-day life, from physical well-being to emotional stability.

C. Untying of the Knots

Many yogic and spiritual concepts create the idea of knots or symbolic errors in the brain's functions that hinder us from understanding our true nature. "Untying of the knots" is a metaphor for enlightenment related to the Kundalini awakening's first stage. In this step, we learn to foster an awareness of what has been hindering us from reconnecting with the primal self which resides deep within our souls. It teaches us how to identify and discard any karma, emotional baggage, or patterns that block us from living life more consciously. By loosening our attachment to all things mental and external, we can tap into inner strength and knowledge, providing liberation through self-illumination. As one reaches Arambha and begins untying their knots, they are devoting themselves to a profound spiritual journey toward every individual's highest truth.

Kriyas and Sequences

One crucial aspect to consider during Arambha is kriyas and sequences. Kriyas are physical movements that can be performed in rhythm or gracefully, depending on the person's preference. They can range from simple rhythmic arm movements to more complicated dance-like body movements. While executing the kriya, one should be conscious of how their breath connects to it and how it affects their overall well-being. Sequences also bring clarity and focus to a practitioner's practice by helping them become more mindful of subtle aspects of their physical practice, such as breathing, calming down of thoughts, and postures. Kriyas and sequences during Arambha play an integral part in facilitating an individual's journey towards Kundalini Awakening.

A. Simple Breathwork-Based Kriya Using Pranayama

Whether you are a beginner or an experienced yogi, simple breathwork-based kriya using pranayama during the first stage of Kundalini awakening can take your practice to the next level. Pranayama is the ancient yogic practice of regulating your breath and increasing prana, which is often referred to as the life force in yoga. Combining pranayama with guided meditation can center your mind and body into a state of higher consciousness so you can tap into the power of Kundalini and experience its healing benefits. Practicing regular kriya during Arambha will assist with developing new levels of mental clarity, self-awareness, and spiritual insight, which can be carried over into all areas of life and bring greater personal growth.

B. Chakra-Activating Sequence with Mantra

A chakra-activating sequence coupled with a mantra is an excellent strategy to maximize the potential of the Arambha stage and keep energy from becoming blocked. During this exercise, you focus on each chakra while visualizing the energies and repeating affirmations to open up your energy centers and create a smooth, balanced flow of universal energy throughout your body. Not only will this technique help you tap into the potential of your Kundalini awakening better, but it can also give you a greater understanding of your center power and offer spiritual guidance as you progress through all stages of awakening.

C. Kundalini Mudra to Activate the Serpent Power

Practicing Kundalini Mudra is an ancient Indian tantric practice designed to awaken the Kundalini energy. Hence, it is used to activate the serpent power during Arambha. It involves the use of hand and body postures, together with a specific breathing technique. Regularly performing this practice can raise their vibrations and energies that eventually cause enlightenment. This meditation practice enables one to achieve awareness of their inner divinity and allows them to better understand their potential. This creates a sense of balance in life which increases vitality and well-being. Practitioners often claim that they experience an increased insight into a deeper understanding of themselves, coupled with a heightened internal connection. Overall, practicing Kundalini Mudra provides physical and spiritual benefits essential for living a healthy life.

Balancing Asanas

One of the most significant parts of Arambha is learning how to include asanas in your practice to promote stillness, grounding, and focus. Balancing asanas uses the concept of counterbalances to find stability both physically and mentally. As practitioners become more comfortable with each pose, they can learn to be mindful and stable while stretching the body's boundaries. Remember that all practices should be tailored specifically for each individual. Balancing asanas should be performed gently and with respect for yourself and your abilities. Arambha can bring you closer to finding harmony within yourself and embracing alignment between your mind, body, and soul.

1. Sun Salutations for Balancing and Renewal

Arambha is the perfect time to reset and recharge, as well as look inward and find balance. Sun salutations are a great way of achieving balanced renewal during this time. This popular yoga practice is traditionally performed at sunrise or right before engaging in any strenuous physical activity. This practice allows us to center ourselves and become re-aligned with our true intention so we feel deeply renewed and balanced. These salutations strengthen our bodies while we are deeply connected with each breath, helping us focus on mental and physical progressive improvement. They involve mantras that serve to both reinvigorate and further calm the mind from all our daily stresses.

2. Corpse Pose to Center and Balance the Mind

The corpse pose is an important position used to center and balance the mind by yoga practitioners of all levels. It is a time to pause during practice and become mindful of present sensations occurring in the body. Many people find the corpse pose to be one of the most difficult postures because it requires total stillness for an extended period. One must make a conscious effort to relax every muscle group, from head to toe, releasing tension from both mind and body. When this posture is practiced correctly, it provides clarity, aids in healing on physical and emotional levels, and brings understanding about how energy naturally flows through the body. Corpse pose is often used at the beginning and end of yoga classes but can work wonders if we dedicate more attention to it, even just five minutes when necessary throughout the day, to re-center and balance the mind that so easily succumbs to stressors in our lives.

3. Seated Poses for Releasing Tension

Before starting any yoga session, take a moment for relaxation and release any built-up tension. Seated poses are some of the best poses for doing this at the start of your practice. In seated poses such as Baddhakonasana (The Cobbler Pose) and Vajrasana (The Thunderbolt Pose), you can gently open up the hips and relax your abdominal muscles. You can also use props such as blocks or blankets to make the posture more comfortable if you're stiff in the hip area. Taking conscious deep breaths while in these poses can further relax your body, improving your ability to move into other poses more effectively. When you are focusing on releasing physical tension, setting an intention also helps you stay focused on that goal during Arambha.

4. Inversions to Connect with the Inner Self

Arambha is a practice that can be seen as an invitation to connect with our inner self and grow through accepting the change. Inversions are essential to this practice, as they can bring about a deeper understanding of oneself and allow for work on any challenging emotions that may arise. Inverting the body is a powerful way to bring about clarity and centering, ultimately allowing us to transform how we experience each moment, create mindful intention and manifest greater joy in our lives. With regular practice, inversions can become an ever-expanding process of connection and liberation within ourselves.

5. Spinal Twists to Rebalance the Chakras

Spinal twists can be performed at the beginning of an Arambha to rebalance your chakras. Starting at the sacrum area, twist your upper body, keeping your hips and pelvis facing forward. This will bring awareness to the powers underlying, supporting, and nourishing you from the ground up. Move up through the vertebrae, twisting through each segment until you reach the C6. Feel the openness between each spinal segment as it moves with grace in a fluid motion. As you twist more deeply into each movement, merging breath with spiritual source energy to connect deeper within, there will be moments where this connection is palpable. Shift mental awareness to focus on that opening and expansiveness while harnessing that power into your physical form. The energy flow has been re-balanced. You stand ready to start your day anew.

Pranayama Practices for Kundalini Activation

Pranayama practices are often recommended for those looking to activate their Kundalini energy. Pranayama is a type of yoga focused on breathing, and since the breath is the cosmic energy that sustains life, it's only natural that using specific breathing techniques to access inner, dormant energy can be beneficial. When practiced regularly, pranayama can help one become more sensitive to their subtle energy fields, such as their chakras, which are thought to be responsible for Kundalini activation. Furthermore, slow and conscious deep breaths calm the mind while releasing toxins from the body. This clears up obstacles that prohibit Kundalini activation.

1. Rhythmic Breathing for Inner Connection

Arambha, the start of something new, can be made even more powerful with some rhythmic breathing. Taking just 10 or 15 seconds to take a deep breath and slowly exhale will allow your body to connect internally with the part of it that is ready for change. This inner connection will bring forth strength and focus, helping you accomplish previously impossible goals. Tune into yourself via rhythmic breathing as you begin this new journey and reap the rewards.

2. Ujjayi Pranayama to Open the Throat Chakra

Ujjayi pranayama is a great way to open the throat chakra during Arambha. This yoga breathing technique involves a low, steady inhalation and exhalation that flows from the center of the chest. It promotes relaxation, removes energy stagnation in the body, and clears residual tension and blocks in the body and mind. The sound generated in Ujjayi pranayama that comes from deep within your throat helps you relax while practicing Arambha while strengthening your cardiovascular system, and aiding with clear communication and problem-solving. Since this type of breathing focuses on awareness of breath flow, it encourages harmony between respiration and physical movement throughout each iteration. Thus, Ujjayi Pranayama can be very helpful in opening up the throat chakra during Arambha, helping us to balance fearlessness in speaking our truth with the vulnerability that it requires.

3. Bhastrika to Stimulate the Nervous System

Executing Bhastrika pranayama is an effective way to stimulate the nervous system. This ancient practice of rhythmic breathing increases oxygen levels, boosts energy, and calms the mind and body. During Bhastrika, your inhalation and exhalation cycle should be done with intention and concentration as they are used to send healing energy throughout the body. It's beneficial when practiced slowly during Arambha because it has a calming effect that relaxes tense muscles so that you can enjoy all of the benefits of the sessions. This practice can also remove toxins from your internal organs while cleansing your bloodstream. Making Bhastrika part of your Kundalini meditation routine is a wonderful way to better receive its therapeutic effects!

4. Sitali Pranayama to Calm the Mind

Sitali Pranayama is a helpful and calming exercise that can be used during the beginning stages of yoga. Sitali Pranayama begins with deep inhales and exhales, curling your tongue and gently rolling and unrolling it while breathing through it. Another part of this exercise is to then take sips from the curled tongue as if drinking water from a spoon or trying to imitate slurping something up. This exercise opens and calms the body, improving other practices such as meditation. It sends a message to both physical and mental states that all is safe in the environment, so there is no need for alarm or worries about external disturbances. Altogether, it imparts a sense of clarity and balance, making it incredibly useful during Arambha when trying to achieve a meditative state or disengage from tension and stress that may exist in the present moment.

5. Brahmari Pranayama for Deep Relaxation

Arambha can be a stressful time for many practitioners of yoga, especially those just starting. That's why deep relaxation is so critical during this period. One beneficial practice to employ is Brahmari Pranayama, or humming bee breath. This breathing exercise quiets the mind and brings mindful awareness to the breath. It also has numerous health benefits, such as lowering stress levels, encouraging better sleep patterns, and calming the central nervous system. The humming sound created during the practice can be incredibly soothing and create a sense of stillness in the body and mind. Regularly practicing Brahmari Pranayama during Arambha can cultivate greater peace, tranquility, and deep relaxation through all stages of their yoga journey.

Closing the Practice

As you come to the end of your practice, allow yourself a few moments to reflect on what you have achieved during your session. Let any emotions or feelings surface, and take note of them without judgment. Notice how you feel physically and mentally, and give thanks for the lessons learned throughout this journey. Spend the last few minutes in stillness, allowing the practice to settle fully, and then slowly open your eyes.

At this point, you have successfully initiated the first stage of Kundalini awakening, Arambha! Through a combination of breathing exercises, pranayama methods, and restorative yoga postures, you have begun the journey toward spiritual growth and self-awareness. With regular practice of these techniques, you can continue to open and develop the chakras triggered during your journey.

The knowledge and insights gained throughout the process are invaluable tools in your spiritual growth, so take time to reflect on all that you have learned. Enjoy this newfound awareness and continue to explore the depths of your inner universe as you journey along the path of Kundalini yoga. Namaste!

Chapter 8: Ghata: Unlocking the Heart Chakra

The next stage in the Kundalini yoga journey is called Ghata, or "the cleansing stage." This phase follows Arambha and is a crucial step towards further spiritual growth. During this stage, practitioners take on an attitude of receiving vast amounts of transformation and healing on all levels to enter their bodies. Completion of the Ghata phase requires patience, dedication, courage, and above all else, an open heart and mind. With these in place, you'll find unity within yourself and your surroundings and the courage to keep exploring the spiritual path.

This chapter will provide an overview of the various aspects of Ghata and how to use Kundalini yoga to reach this stage. It will explain what happens during Ghata, the chakras affected and their effects, and the kriyas and sequences for reaching this stage. Asanas and pranayama practices for Ghata will also be discussed, as well as how to close the practice. The information in this chapter is meant to be an introduction and a general understanding of the Ghata phase.

Ghata: The Cleansing Stage

The ancient practice of Kundalini awakening has been slowly gaining popularity in modern-day spiritual circles. The cleansing stage of this process, often called Ghata, is an essential step in awakening your internal wisdom and power. Ghata is all about purifying the body and mind to prepare for the ascension of energy taking place within the body. This includes deep breathing exercises, chanting mantras, clearing the mind of any negative thoughts, and visualization exercises. Once the cleansing phase has been completed, the journey toward spiritual strength can truly begin. Ghata is vital in awakening your Kundalini energy and should not be missed on many paths to enlightenment.

A. What Happens during Ghata

Kundalini energy begins to rise through the seven chakras, and old beliefs and unhealthy habits are cleared away as it progresses. This can cause various physical and mental effects, from tingling sensations throughout the body to waves of intense emotion. People often experience heightened self-awareness during this time, allowing for deeper insight into their thoughts and feelings. Although Ghata can be uncomfortable at first, working through it with mindful awareness provides great clarity and insight – a key element on the path of spiritual growth.

B. Chakras Affected and Their Effects

Ghata, or the cleansing stage of Kundalini awakening, can affect each of the seven chakras throughout the body. The root chakra, at the base of the spine, is cleansed to open us up to abundant energy and support. The sacral chakra is cleared for emotional openness and proper creative flow. The solar plexus chakra is purified to allow us unyielding confidence and determination.

The heart chakra is enlightened to create powerful love and empathy within us. The throat chakra is opened, increasing communication and honest self-expression. Lastly, the third eye chakra gains clarity generating greater intuition along with sharper mental focus, while the crown chakra becomes more connected to the divine, allowing spiritual awakening. During Ghata, all of the chakras are affected, creating balance within and manifesting great growth and wisdom within us.

C. Untying of the Knots

Dissolving the knots of energy through Ghata is a critical process in activating Kundalini. It creates a ripple effect throughout the body and soul, making our natural energy flow substantially uncongested. This can create a powerful sense of awareness and clarity, as chakras may respond in a way that was not previously possible. The kriyas or practices used during this stage gradually uncoil these tightly knotted energies to further awaken consciousness on a higher level. This can benefit various aspects of life, such as emotional balancing, physical well-being, and spiritual growth. Furthermore, it unlocks your full potential so you can take your true path toward fulfillment more clearly and vigorously.

Kriyas and Sequences for the Ghata Stage

In yoga, the Ghata stage is a strength-building portion of practice that focuses on activating and integrating body systems. A few of the great tools for this work are kriyas and sequences. *Kriyas* involve extending postures with repetitions or alternating sequences. These sequences put poses together in a way that gives rise to ever-deepening layers of experience as you move through them, from a physical challenge into full mental/physical integration. With regular practice of kriyas and sequences, we can develop flexibility, strength, endurance, and focus that help us move beyond the boundaries of our current level of ability into something entirely new.

1. Uddiyana Bandha

Yoga practitioners often use Uddiyana Bandha to remove physical tension and tightness while mental blocks are cleared away. Generally achieved in the standing position, Uddiyana Bandha is the practice of sucking the navel area inward towards the spine. This "engaging" of our bodies creates a sudden rush of energy, balancing the flow within us and facilitating further cleansing during Kundalini awakening. It also builds internal heat and reduces stress in the abdominal area while controlling our breath through conscious inhalation and exhalation. The practice cleanses our systems more thoroughly during Ghata, allowing for an even stronger connection to our highest selves when we reach the next stage in Kundalini awakening.

2. Nauli

Nauli Kriya is a powerful cleansing ritual commonly practiced in the Ghata stage of the Kundalini awakening. It works to expel stagnant energy and toxins within the body, simultaneously encouraging new vitality. Through abdominal muscle contractions, practitioners can strengthen their core and sacral chakras, allowing energy to move freely through the system. This encourages clarity in the physical body and is a gateway to deeper levels of self-awareness. Nauli kriya offers both liberation and transformation as participants get to know themselves more deeply, sparking immense healing on a spiritual level.

3. Agni Sara

Ghata, the cleansing stage of the Kundalini awakening, can often be an energy-consuming process. To help revitalize your energy and quicken the cleansing process, many practitioners have turned to Agni Sara Kriya. This energizing pranayama exercise cleanses the internal organs while working the core abdominal muscles, stimulating the manifestation of Kundalini energy. It's commonly recommended as a great practice to accompany any sort of Kundalini work or meditation you may be undertaking. Ultimately, Agni Sara Kriya is a wonderful tool for anyone looking to maximize their Ghata practice and further activate their full spiritual potential.

4. Kumbhaka

Kumbhaka kriya is a powerful meditation practice aimed at clearing out any energetic blockages in the body, allowing for an open channel and better flow of life force energy. During this stage, focus on the energy centers within you while holding your breath. You also focus on prana, or life force, and aim to bring fresh and vital energy into your being that helps create mental clarity, spiritual connection, and improved overall well-being. Practitioners usually begin with shorter periods of breath holds to gain mastery over it before attempting longer breaths with practice and dedication. The goal is to take long breaths without feeling uncomfortable and eventually progress into even deeper states of pranayama, which brings greater clarity and presence.

5. Kapalabhati

The Kapalabhati technique enables one to fine-tune their prana, or vital life-force energy, throughout their body. This work is done through a special type of breathing known as Kapalabhati pranayama. Also called "shining skull breath," it clears out toxins from the organism and balances energies within the body. As this process happens, your physical and spiritual well-being will start to improve and release blockages along all energy pathways, allowing for a powerful Kundalini awakening. With continued practice, you'll feel spiritually invigorated with each inhalation and exhalation of breath, connecting you to the divine source within you.

Asanas for Ghata

Asanas are a series of postures and breathing exercises also designed to cleanse the mind and body. This stage is the start of a journey towards union with source energy. Each asana detoxifies us at the physical and energetic level, gently pushing our minds and bodies into harmony so that we can move through each blockage in our transformation process. Moving through this self-nurturing practice calms the nervous system and strengthens both mental clarity and emotional resilience. After completing these exercises, practitioners often feel energized, peaceful, and deeply centered in themselves. Ghata focuses on creating a balance between movement and stillness so that you feel restored to your true state of being, an elevated connection to the divine energy that brings more happiness to life's difficult moments.

1. Ustrasana

Ustrasana is a demanding asana that focuses on releasing stagnant energy involuntarily stored in your body associated with unresolved memories, suppressed emotions, and trauma. This asana is performed by lying on your back, bending the knee, and bringing it close to your chest while lifting the hips and extending the arms upwards. Ustrasana is a powerful exercise that helps clear out any blockages in our energetic pathways, allowing for more peaceful energy to flow through us.

In addition to the energetic cleanse, Ustrasana provides the physical strength gained from the deep stretching and strengthening within postures like this one that strengthens us physically and mentally for facing future challenges. For those looking to unlock the transformative power of Kundalini yoga, Ustrasana for Ghata can be a foundational pillar of practice in a customized program.

2. Bhujangasana

Practicing Bhujangasana or "Cobra Pose" is an excellent way to begin the Ghata stage. This pose awakens and energizes the spine while opening up blocked energy along the spine. It encourages the full expansion of breath in the body, allowing one to elevate your consciousness. To enter the posture, lie on your stomach and then slowly lift your chest off the floor while arching your back and keeping your legs on the ground.

The cobra pose will help open up any blocked energy along the spine, allowing a more free-flowing flow of prana throughout the body. With an open and clear mind, Bhujangasana can also effectively purify old emotions that no longer serve you, making way for new energies to emerge. In sum, if you are starting your own Kundalini awakening journey, don't forget to make Bhujangasana your companion!

3. Adho Mukha Svanasana

If you want to improve your overall health and connect with your Kundalini energy, Adho Mukha Svanasana is a great place to start. Also known as the Downward-Facing Dog Pose, this powerful combination of stretching and breathing can help accelerate the cleansing stage in Kundalini awakening. To perform this pose, start on all fours and slowly press your hips into the air while straightening your arms and legs.

Holding this posture for a few minutes helps promote full body detoxification and stimulate the body's energy pathways. This posture can also strengthen digestion, reduce fatigue, and open up any blockages in the spine. Practicing this pose regularly can help improve one's overall health and well-being, making it an essential practice for those striving towards Ghata in their Kundalini awakening journey.

4. Salabasana

The practice of Salabasana for Ghata, or the cleansing stage of Kundalini awakening, has been used for centuries in yogic traditions. It is a powerful technique used to clear stagnant energy from the body and mind, which can arise from physical or mental health issues. To perform this exercise properly, one should move into the posture with deep breaths and stay there for at least five minutes. First, start by lying on your stomach and slowly lift your chest off the floor while arching your back. Doing this opens up any blockages that may be present in our energy pathways.

As the energy starts to flow freely, a feeling of light begins to spread through the body. An increased sense of inner peace follows this as blockages are cleared away. Mentally and emotionally, one can feel energized and uplifted due to the transformation in energy flow throughout the body. All of this culminates in a greater sense of self-awareness and deeper connection with one's inner divine potential that all yogis strive towards, making Salabasana for Ghata both a spiritually enriching and fulfilling experience.

5. Setubandhasana

By practicing Setubandhasana, you can unlock the dormant Kundalini energy within yourself and awaken its true potential. This asana, sometimes called *the bridge pose*, clears energetic blockages from the body and cultivates a heightened level of spirituality. To perform the pose properly, you must begin by sitting comfortably on the ground with your knees bent and your feet placed flat on either side of your hips.

Ensure that your spine remains straight as you slowly begin to arch upward, gradually lifting your hips until your legs and torso make a "bridge" shape before returning to the starting position. As you practice this pose more often, you may notice a gradual increase in energy that brings with it improved clarity of thought and tranquility in lifestyle choices.

Pranayama Practices for Ghata

Ghata is about cleansing and purifying the energy field for us to be ready to take on the journey ahead. Pranayama resets our system, making it more receptive to the spiritual energy that awaits us. These practices range from breathwork to mantra chanting and visualization. Each practice has its energy associated with it, allowing us to connect with our inner power and open our chakras up for growth. Pranayama also increases our vital life force, which can, in turn, give us the strength to enhance and deepen our spiritual experiences. Despite being a critical aspect of Kundalini awakening, these practices are easy and beneficial for anyone who wants to reconnect with the divine within.

1. Nadi Shodhana

Nadi Shodhana Pranayama is an essential practice for the Ghata, or the cleansing stage, of the Kundalini awakening. This pranayama effectively cleanses the subtle energy channels and improves their health. Through this practice, we may experience intense feelings of joy, contentment, and peace that come from removing blockages in our energetic bodies. You can practice Nadi Shodhana Pranayama anywhere since no specific space or equipment is necessary.

Begin by sitting comfortably and then shifting your attention inward to focus on your breath. Allow your inhales and exhales to become long and slow as you move through this gentle practice. As you continue to practice the Nadi Shodhana Pranayama regularly, you will notice significant improvements in your mental and emotional well-being.

2. Anuloma Viloma

Anuloma Viloma Pranayama releases blockages and imbalances for the practitioner to take part in more advanced forms of meditation. During this practice, the individual inhales through one nostril and exhales through another in a continuous pattern. They hold their breath briefly before beginning a new cycle. Anuloma Viloma purifies the *nadis* (energy channels) and increases their permeability to allow higher levels of *prana* (energy) to flow freely throughout the body. It also aids in de-stressing, clarity of thought, and relaxation, making it a beneficial practice for everyone regardless of whether Kundalini awakening is desired or not.

3. Bhramari

Bhramari Pranayama is an ancient breathing technique used in Kundalini yoga to help the practitioner achieve Ghata, the cleansing stage of the Kundalini awakening. This unique and powerful tool clears out physical and mental debris and opens up prana (life force) pathways within the body, allowing energy to flow more freely. The practice involves inhaling deeply through the nose while simultaneously pressing on the tragus, a small protrusion on the earlobe. At the same time, a gentle humming sound is generated inwardly to energize and balance all seven chakras. Remember that practitioners must use self-regulation when practicing Bhramari Pranayama as it can become quite intense, so don't be afraid to take breaks or reduce intensities as needed.

Regardless of the stage of your Kundalini awakening, always end the practice with a sense of gratitude. Thank yourself for taking the time to reconnect with your spiritual self and be present at that moment. Bring awareness to any changes you may have noticed throughout the Ghata stage and take some time to integrate those into your life. This is an essential part of the process, allowing you to honor and appreciate your inner journey. Take a few deep breaths, open your eyes, and slowly return to your physical body. Finally, take some time to sit in silence and allow any lingering energetic shifts or feelings to settle completely within your being. Namaste!

Chapter 9: Pacihaya And Nishpatti: Unlocking Your Crown

Once you've moved through the first two stages of Kundalini awakening, you can move on to the next two stages of this journey, Pacihaya and Nishpatti. Pacihaya is the absorption stage where Kundalini energy moves throughout the whole body instead of just focusing on particular chakras. Nishpatti is the final stage of awakening and marks a massive shift in consciousness. This chapter will discuss the different kriyas and practices you can do to experience Pacihaya and Nishpatti. The Pacihaya and Nishpatti stages of Kundalini awakening are both crucial for reaching the highest states of spiritual consciousness. So, let's dive into what you need to know about these stages.

Pacihaya: The Absorption Stage

Pacihaya, otherwise known as the absorption stage of Kundalini awakening, is a significant part of spiritual development. During this stage, practitioners allow themselves to fully absorb and integrate newfound spiritual knowledge as they journey further along their chosen path. Access to Pacihaya can be through rituals, meditations, or even more intense techniques such as yoga or pranayama breathing exercises. One's ability to reach this state of understanding lies in trusting the power of universal energy to guide you and help you explore unfamiliar depths within yourself. When done correctly, this practice can bring about a transcendent sense of enlightenment, compassion for all living beings, unconditional love for oneself and others, and a connection with the divine realms.

A. What Happens during Pacihaya

Pacihaya, or the absorption stage of Kundalini awakening, describes the remarkable process when an individual becomes aware of their connection to their true self and ultimately to a higher form of divine power. During this phase of spiritual growth, individuals can experience anything from raising energy in their body's spine as emotion-filled energy to removing layers of inhibition and fear that were blocking pathways to joy.

Many in this phase often talk about inner tranquility and physical sensations that help them reach new heights of awareness. Along with profound feelings, strong visuals and higher mental clarity can accompany Pacihaya as the individual moves towards heightened spiritual understanding. In essence, the absorption stage is a beautiful moment in life where one can begin discovering more meaningful insight into the bigger picture around them, creating opportunities for expanded growth in a spiritual realm.

B. Chakras Affected and Their Effects

The energy of a Kundalini awakening is intense and can cause an intoxicating array of sensations. Pacihaya involves the mind drawing energy from various chakras as it progresses. The lower chakras will draw in physical energies such as passion and divine love, whereas the upper chakras absorb emotional energies like clarity and joy. During this process, there may be feelings of trembling and surging, as well as psychosomatic disturbances. Through this process, however, people reach a heightened state of consciousness, allowing them to tap into profound levels of awareness not experienced during the normal flow of everyday life.

C. How Pacihaya Is Different from Other Stages

How the energy of Pacihaya is experienced is different from that of other Kundalini awakening stages as it does not move from one main chakra to another as the other stages do. Rather, it spreads throughout the entire body from its point of origin in the heart chakra. This is why it is known as the absorption stage – since its purpose is to allow practitioners to absorb and integrate newfound spiritual knowledge instead of just traveling from one chakra to the next.

Kundalini Kriyas to Trigger Pacihaya

Kundalini kriyas are powerful, breath-based exercises designed to help activate and open our energy channels so that Kundalini energy can be released and expand throughout the body. These kriyas, when performed correctly, will enable us to reach the Pacihaya state during a Kundalini awakening. Pacihaya is an energized resting stage where we absorb the potent vibrations from the awakened energy and integrate them with our spiritual awareness.

To achieve this calming yet liberating feeling, it's crucial to incorporate breathing exercises, visualization techniques like focusing on a healing color such as blue or purple, gentle movements like swaying back and forth or spinning around in circles, and mantra chanting that clears out negative mental energies. When practiced consistently, these kriyas will lead you on a journey to deeper levels of connection with your inner self, one in which you feel enlightened and ready for whatever comes next.

1. Sat Kriya

Sat Kriya is an ancient technique that works in the energetic realm to connect a person's physical and spiritual bodies. Performing Sat Kriya has been hailed as possibly the most effective tool for initiating Pacihaya, the absorption stage of Kundalini awakening. This mystical practice opens up one's energy systems, enabling a more powerful and integrated connection with our inner wisdom and divine nature.

The practice involves channeling pranic (life force) energy up and down the spine, affecting both the physical and subtle bodies while producing peaceful mental states that lead to profound inner transformation. Sat Kriya, along with other techniques, can be helpful during Pacihaya, thus allowing individuals to imbibe divine energy into their bodies to experience greater gains in awareness and meaningful shifts in consciousness.

2. Om Chanting

Om chanting is increasingly being used to trigger the absorption stage of Kundalini awakening. By focusing your energy on the sound of Om and repeating it as you meditate, you can awaken the dormant source of Kundalini's power within you. Generally, if this stage is successful, those who have done it can experience an infusion of spiritual energy throughout their body and mind. Beyond leading to higher levels of consciousness, this heightened awareness can open pathways for creative insight and profound understanding. Om chanting is a powerful tool for unlocking our inner potential and helps us move one step closer to enlightenment.

3. Surrender and Breathwork

Breathwork and surrender are two seemingly opposite approaches to experiencing the absorption stage of Kundalini awakening. To experience Pacihaya, both must be part of your practice, allowing yourself to breathe deeply with awareness and consciously giving up control. With each deep breath, we cultivate a deeper level of relaxation in our body and mind. As we increasingly relax into our natural state of surrender, we start recognizing the inner power that brings greater clarity in both thought and emotion through the acceptance and appreciation of all life has to offer. When we can make these conscious connections, our Pacihaya journey begins as we move toward understanding our true potential as spiritual beings in an energy-filled world.

4. Khechari Mudra

Khechari Mudra, a powerful practice for activating the inner spiritual potential in yoga, is said to be pivotal in triggering Pacihaya, the absorption stage of the Kundalini awakening. This mudra involves pressing your tongue upward toward the soft palate while gently double-rolling it backward and sealing it against the uvula. This complex process unleashes energy that can be directed via awareness toward any chakra. When done regularly, perception and understanding of deep, underlying energy fields truly amplify. In addition to physical benefits such as improved digestion and better overall health, this mudra brings clarity to all areas of life, providing a sense of balance that empowers one with greater mental capacity and focus.

5. Bandhas

To get to the Pacihaya stage, one must train their body and mind to push through blockages so that vital energy can flow freely. One way to do this is by using bandhas exercises. Bandhas involve contracting certain muscles which redirect prana, or life force energy. Try holding the *mula bandha*, or root lock, engaging your pelvic floor muscles and pulling them up. Similarly, to practice *nauli*, you need to first contract your abdominal muscles and then isolate certain sections of the abdomen by further contracting certain regions with a circular motion. This activates the solar plexus chakra, which is connected to our

Kundalini energy. Once practiced regularly, bandhas unblock energy pathways that are inhibiting our spiritual growth and allow us to progress further into the Pacihaya stage.

Nishpatti: The Final Stage

Nishpatti is the final stage of elevating consciousness and tapping into the immense power that lies deep within. This ultimately leads to a deeper insight into truths and an intensified connection with one's inner being. During this process, various mental, emotional, and physical breakdowns are experienced as higher states of awareness are met. It marks an enlightening step in life as the awakened Kundalini energy brings about self-realization and liberation from the mundane cycles of life. It is an undeniably powerful experience for those brave enough to embark on this journey of self-discovery as they ultimately unlock their spiritual potential.

A. What to Expect during Nishpatti

In the final stage of Kundalini's awakening, you'll no longer be guided by any force outside of itself and instead gain an absolute connection with your energy. As the energy ascends, you'll feel a heightened sense of self-awareness and a deep understanding of the world surrounding you. Furthermore, this state of being can bring immense joy and contentment as you come to understand yourself on a more meaningful level. During Nishpatti, stay open to whatever unfolds in the inner journey and use healing practices such as meditation to further enhance the connection with your true self.

B. Consciousness Expansion

Consciousness expansion during Nishpatti, the final stage of the Kundalini awakening, is an incredibly special experience. It is often called a state of enlightenment and oneness with the universe. During this period, one's awareness of oneself and the world around you is much more expanded. This greater sense of understanding can help you connect more meaningfully with other people and become more attuned to their internal needs. It also gives practitioners a better appreciation for the beauty in our world, helping us see life from a higher perspective. Ultimately, the state of consciousness expansion that comes during Nishpatti can offer an incredible sense of balance, peace, and insight into our true inner selves.

Kundalini Kriyas to Trigger Nishpatti

In Kundalini yoga, kriyas are used to trigger the final stage of the Kundalini awakening. This process involves spiritual self-realization and promises peace of mind and body to attain a higher consciousness. A variety of kriyas can be used during this process, from meditation, chanting mantras, and spiritual breathing exercises. To reach the highest level is to stay disciplined with your practice by being consistent and focused. The journey is different for each individual, as every person has their own way of working through struggles and achieving liberation. All these factors come together through practicing Kundalini kriyas so that the ultimate goal, triggering Nishpatti, can finally be attained.

1. Pranayama

Pranayama is an indispensable tool for those seeking to awaken their Kundalini energy. It is said that by mastering this yogic practice, we can come one step closer to reaching the final stage of Kundalini awakening. Pranayama consists of rhythmic and continual breath control whereby we can send fresh oxygen and vital energy throughout our body and clear any blockages hindering the ascension of our Kundalini. This type of breath work also promotes balance within our body and mind, further assisting in the activation of Kundalini. Thus, with sufficient practice and dedication, we can reach Nishpatti's sublime state through Pranayama, where true liberation awaits us.

2. Mantra Meditation

Mantra meditation is one of the most effective methods for triggering Kundalini awakening. By focusing intently on a powerful and meaningful mantra or sound, a person can tap into their higher inner potential and eventually experience the ultimate stage of spiritual transformation. This process works best when done in an atmosphere of peace, stillness, and awareness. It also requires perseverance, dedication, and total devotion to reach a "state of consciousness beyond all duality." Ultimately, this type of spiritual practice connects individuals to their inner divinity, enabling them to attain true enlightenment.

3. Visualization and Affirmations

Learning how to trigger Nishpatti through visualization and affirmations is a powerful way to become more attuned to your spiritual growth. Visualization is a type of meditation that can guide us in accessing our inner realms, while affirmations are conscious statements of the truth we want to embody and the purpose we have chosen for ourselves from within our deepest being. When used together, visualizations and affirmations can empower us to realize our mind-body-soul and tap into deeper levels of consciousness for greatness. Visualization directs our energy toward what we desire most, while affirmations provide repeated confirmation that reinforces the power of this sacred process. With practice, anyone can learn techniques for visualization and affirmations to trigger Nishpatti, ultimately helping their manifest destiny come alive.

4. Kundalini Yoga Postures

Kundalini positions are an effective way to open the blocks that stand in the way of Kundalini awakening. When used with skill, they can be effective tools to help the practitioner reach Nishpatti. Through practice, one can use these postures to clear energy blockages, activate physical, emotional, and mental healing, and restore vitality and clarity to one's life. Examples of postures beneficial for triggering Nishpatti are deep abdominal breathing, spinal twists, shoulder stands, cat-cow stretches, Vajrasana or "thunderbolt squat" posture, meditation practices such as mantra chanting, and more. Each posture has its purpose and impact on achieving higher self-awareness. You can move into a full spiritual awakening with practice, patience, and perseverance.

5. Pratyahara

Pratyahara, the act of internal concentration and withdrawal from external engagement or activities, is an essential step to trigger Nishpatti. This practice develops greater powers of focus, which lead to a heightened state of spiritual awareness and helps to raise dormant energies through the body. Through regular practice of Pratyahara, one tunes into their inner energy and can then elevate that energy to higher levels. Furthermore, by engaging in this level of self-discovery, practitioners experience insights into their own spiritual identity and come closer to mastering inner peace. Pratyahara sets you up for Kundalini awakening and allows you to experience inner realms of pure bliss and divine realization during your journey.

Kundalini awakening is a powerful phenomenon that requires dedication and patience, but with the right techniques and practices, such as visualization and affirmations, postures, and Pratyahara, you can reach the ultimate stage of the Kundalini awakening. Regular practice allows one to become more connected to their inner being and mobilize energies within the body to better understand the divine and the self. With this newfound awareness, you can experience a profound transformation and move closer to fully awakening your Kundalini energy.

Chapter 10: Kundalini Energy Is Awakened, Now What?

Kundalini awakening can be an intense and sometimes overwhelming experience, as it is a process of spiritual growth involving major shifts in consciousness. By understanding the process and having access to the right resources and guidance, you can accept and lead a happy life with your expanded consciousness. Experiencing a Kundalini awakening can be life-changing, but it doesn't always come without consequences. When an individual's Kundalini energy is awakened to the point where it is overactive, it can cause physical and emotional discomfort, making it difficult for them to adjust to and cope with the effects.

Often intertwined with intense spiritual experience, overactive Kundalini can be overwhelming and stress the body and mind too much. In this chapter, we will advise how to accept your new consciousness and offer Kundalini yoga kriyas, techniques, and sequences to tame an overactive Kundalini. Finally, we will discuss calming techniques to help you adjust if your Kundalini awakening was unintentional. This chapter aims to help you gain confidence in managing your Kundalini energy and living a fulfilling life with it.

Accept Your New Consciousness

The awakening of your Kundalini energy is a special and powerful experience. It can be difficult to let go of the beliefs and mental patterns you have accustomed to, but it is worth it. Once your Kundalini energy is awakened, you have been given a chance to grow into something new, something beautiful and expanded in consciousness. Accepting your new self is key to fully utilizing the potential that this life-changing transformation has unlocked within you. Allow yourself to explore and find comfort in any shifts, recognitions, or personal discoveries you may encounter on this journey of self-discovery.

Kundalini Yoga Kriyas to Tame an Overactive Kundalini

An overactive Kundalini is an alarming condition for many who seek spiritual development. Without proper guidance and understanding of the energy's reactiveness, it can have devastating effects on your emotional, physical, and psychological health. The entirety of the individual will be subjected to the intense vibrations generated by an overactive Kundalini that can cause a range of physiological symptoms, from anxiety and sleeplessness to lack of clarity in thoughts and hyperactivity. The flow of uncontrolled energy can easily put too much strain on the body, making it turbulent. Here are some Kundalini yoga kriyas and techniques which you can use to tame an overactive Kundalini.

1. Heart Chakra Meditation

In times of chaos, it can be difficult to find peace. One way to do so is through heart chakra meditation. This practice calms and balances the Kundalini energy at the spine's base. By grounding yourself in the present moment with deep breathing exercises and visualizations, you can inspire a sense of peacefulness throughout your mind and body while harnessing your life force energy. Heart chakra meditation also brings intention into each movement and helps us to cultivate self-love as we accept our current circumstances.

To begin, sit comfortably with your spine erect and your legs crossed. Close your eyes and bring awareness to the heart chakra located at the center of your chest. Visualize a white light radiating from the center of your chest and extending outwards in all directions. Focus on the breath as you inhale and exhale deeply, allowing your body to relax more with every inhalation and exhalation. With continued practice, we can begin to overcome everyday struggles and create harmony within ourselves and our environment.

2. Breath Awareness

There are many complex pathways to self-awareness, but breath awareness is always essential for unlocking dormant energies like the Kundalini. By using slow, deep breaths and focusing on the sensation of air flowing through the body, you'll enter a meditative state that may soothe and excite your innermost consciousness. While this alone does not result in the awakening of Kundalini, it serves as a platform for one's spirit to travel and seek peace within you. This process requires patience, love, and discipline but can bring forth greatness in terms of spiritual growth and understanding of inner power. So let go with breath awareness, reach out with your awareness, and access an enlightened way of living.

3. Mantra Japa

Mantra Japa is a centuries-old, powerful spiritual practice that tames an overactive Kundalini. In this practice, the individual chants sacred mantras and syllables out loud or in their minds, repeating them with intention and focus. Through this practice, deeper layers of their unconscious are accessed and energized. It works to bring balance by activating the chakras, which can ground and center an overexcited Kundalini. Anyone looking to find stillness in their Kundalini energy should try Mantra Japa. Its calming effect can be felt almost immediately, leading to an overall sense of peace, happiness, and well-being.

4. Asanas and Mudras

A range of yoga poses and mudras can tame an overactive Kundalini. These involve carefully placing the body into specific poses and mudras, which activate the subtle energies of the body. Asanas and mudras focus on particular energetic points to direct the flow of energy, aiding in releasing any blockages or constraints that may be keeping the Kundalini from achieving balance. Here are some poses which can be used for this purpose:

- **Gomukhasana (Cow Face Pose):** This pose calms the mind and body by releasing tension from the shoulders and neck. It also helps stimulate the central nervous system and the endocrine glands.

- **Baddha Konasana (Butterfly Pose):** This pose stretches the inner thighs and opens up the hip area. It also brings an overall sense of relaxation to the body.

- **Matsyasana (Fish Pose):** This pose strengthens the spine and opens up the chest area. It also reduces fatigue and stress by calming the mind.
- **Ardha Matsyendrasana (Half Lord of the Fishes Pose):** This pose reduces stress and fatigue by stimulating the spine, hips, abdomen, and chest area.
- **Padmasana (Lotus Pose):** This pose calms the mind and body by releasing tension from the hips and legs. It also helps to stimulate the central nervous system.
- **Pran Mudra:** This mudra balances the energy flow in the body and brings a sense of focus and clarity.

Sequences to Tame an Overactive Kundalini

Uncontrolled activation of Kundalini can hurt the body and mind. To regulate it, special sequences of breath work and postures have been created to help tame an overactive Kundalini. These sequences are designed to awaken clear energy paths in the body and balance out energy levels, restoring balance and harmony in both body and soul. With regular practice, these sequences can bring tangible results and help open the door to deeper states of consciousness.

1. Balancing Sequence

Balancing the flow of Kundalini energy throughout the body is critical for mental and physical health. The correct sequence of yoga poses can help achieve this balance without injury or strain. Forward bends are a calming yoga pose that can strengthen muscles, relax the mind, and bring awareness to the spine. Backbends engage and strengthen the heart center, reversing any blockages in energetic pathways, followed by twists that flush out any toxins and create more flexibility in the spine. Finally, inversions provide many benefits, like reducing stress levels and boosting alertness. Regularly following this sequence of forward bends, backbends, twists, and inversions can maintain the natural flow of Kundalini energy throughout your body.

2. Kundalini Awakening Sequence

This sequence is designed to awaken the Kundalini and create a deep connection between body and soul. To start, Nadi Shodhan Pranayama, a traditional breathing technique, can be used to balance the nervous system and awaken the chakras. It is followed by Surya Namaskar, or

Sun Salutations, which helps build heat in the body and create an energy flow from head to toe. The next step is to do a series of asanas and mudras to open up the blocked energy points in the body, allowing Kundalini to rise. Finally, meditation can calm the mind and allow for an effortless connection with divine wisdom.

3. Chakra Cleansing Sequence

The chakras are energy centers that need to be balanced and cleansed regularly. This sequence is designed to open, clear, and balance the chakras throughout the body. Grounding poses like Tadasana (Mountain Pose) can be used to connect with the Earth's energy. Ujjayi Pranayama can be used to bring awareness and clarity to the mind. Next, a series of asanas can be used to activate each chakra. Finally, meditation can cleanse the chakras and create space for inner stillness.

4. Prana Vayu Balancing Sequence

Prana Vayu is the life force energy that flows through the body and helps maintain health. This sequence is designed to open up a stuck Prana, promote a healthy flow of life force energy throughout the body and bring balance and harmony. To start, Nadi Shodhan Pranayama can create an even flow of energy throughout the body. A series of standing, seated, and inverted poses can open up all the energy centers in the body. Finally, meditation can be used to unite with Universal energies and promote a lasting sense of well-being.

By practicing these sequences regularly, you'll experience a deeper connection between your physical and energetic bodies allowing for a healthier, happier life. Remember to always take your time when practicing and listen to what your body is telling you, as it will guide you toward the best path for self-discovery.

Calming an Unintended Kundalini Awakening

Kundalini awakening can be both an exciting and a terrifying experience. The energy unlocked through this phenomenon can be very strong and even lead to trance-like states of consciousness if left unchecked. However, while some people seek out Kundalini awakenings intentionally, there are many whose awakenings happen unintentionally and can be difficult to manage.

Fortunately, yoga practitioners have developed techniques to calm an unintended Kundalini awakening, such as focusing on breathwork or visualizing the energy connecting different chakras in your body. Meditation is also helpful in lowering stress levels and allowing the energetic waves to safely ease out of one's body. Other activities, such as yoga poses and physical or creative outlets, may be beneficial when managing an unintended Kundalini awakening.

A. Preparing the Body and Mind

When Kundalini energy is awakened, it can cause increased physical and mental arousal, which can be quite uncomfortable. Relaxation techniques such as yoga, breathwork, and meditation are recommended to prepare the body and mind for a calm and peaceful state. This allows us to clear energetic blockages from our energy centers in the body which supports the information needed for calming an unintended Kundalini awakening. Mindfulness can also play a crucial role in preparation as it brings awareness to our thoughts and feelings accompanying the process. By implementing steps that address physiological and psychological needs, we can create a safe space necessary for achieving a well-balanced state of inner peace.

B. Grounding Techniques

To quell the intensity of a Kundalini experience, grounding techniques are beneficial in calming the process. These techniques involve focusing on the senses, such as feeling the contact of one's feet on solid ground or hands saturating in cold water. One could also focus on something outside themselves, such as a tree with its roots firmly planted in the earth. All of these techniques bring attention back to the body and away from any other mental distractions that might arise during an unintended awakening. Using grounding techniques will bring a sense of safety and a level of control that aids in successfully navigating bouts of intense energy.

C. Releasing Stored Negative Energy

Releasing stored negative energy is essential to calming an unintended Kundalini awakening. Kundalini is healing energy within all of us, but if it is released too quickly or without proper guidance, it can bring up issues that we never even knew were there. That's why releasing stored negative energy properly is so critical. Breathing, yoga, and meditation are just a few ways to accomplish this.

Taking the time to be mindful and connect with yourself on a deeper level can help you rid yourself of any underlying blocks or tension held within your body and spirit. Kundalini knows no bounds, but with respect and dedication, it can create positive results in our lives. Moving through the process of releasing stored negative energy with self-love and compassion can bring rhythm and balance back into our lives and make our relationship with Kundalini more powerful than ever before.

D. Connecting with Nature

Being in nature is a powerful and calming method to address an unintended Kundalini awakening. It reminds us of the interconnectedness of all life and our surroundings and gives us a sense of connection to something greater than ourselves. The beauty of nature can provide insight into oneself, bringing clarity to the inner turmoil created by the Kundalini process. Taking slow, mindful walks in nature allows us to be present in each moment, from the shape of leaves to the sound of birds singing or the feeling of soil beneath our feet. Being conscious of our senses allows us to look inward for understanding as we navigate this unexpected journey of physical, emotional, and spiritual transformation.

E. Connecting with Others

Connecting with others when trying to calm an unintended Kundalini awakening can also work well. Working closely with a spiritual advisor, healer, or coach can help you focus your energy on ways to cope and create inner balance. Sharing insights and stories, such as dreams and symbols related to Kundalini energy patterns, is also a great way to gain clarity amid an experience that may sometimes feel chaotic and overwhelming. This can help you develop insight into the root causes of the awakening to more fully appreciate and understand it. Moreover, talking and listening with other people who have gone through similar experiences can be empowering. Ultimately, connecting with others who are familiar with Kundalini energy allows us to share a feeling of solidarity as we journey through this transformative process.

The journey of Kundalini awakening can be intense and chaotic, but with the right tools and practices, we can learn to navigate it more gracefully. By grounding ourselves, releasing stored negative energy, connecting with nature, and connecting with others who understand the process, we can find a sense of clarity within the storm. This process ultimately allows us to discover our core power and potential, creating a harmonious relationship with this mysterious energy. Accepting and embracing the journey of Kundalini awakening is an act of courage that can lead to a profound transformation in our lives.

Glossary of Terms

Several Hindu terms and concepts related to Kundalini have been used throughout this book. For reference, here is an alphabetized list of these terms and their meanings or English translations.

Agni: Fire, used to describe the Kundalini force rising through the chakras

Ajna: Also known as the third eye, it is located between the eyebrows and is considered a major energy center.

Anahata: Another major energy center situated in the chest and associated with the heart.

Arambha: The first stage of awakening the Kundalini energy

Ardha Matsyendrasana: Half Lord of the Fishes Pose, a yoga posture used to stimulate the Kundalini

Asana: Yoga posture

Chakra: The circular energy centers along the spine of a practitioner, each with its color and purpose

Drishti: A focused gaze used in certain yoga postures

Ghata: The cleansing stage of Kundalini awakening, followed right after Arambha.

Kriya: A series of yoga poses, breathing exercises, and meditation practices used to activate the Kundalini

Kundalini: The spiritual energy located at the base of the spine that can be activated through yoga and meditation

Mantra: A sacred sound or phrase used for meditation and spiritual development

Manipura: The third chakra, located in the navel area and associated with confidence and self-esteem

Mudra: A symbolic hand gesture used in yoga and meditation

Muladhara: The root chakra at the base of the spine

Nadi: An energy channel

Nishpatti: The final stage of awakening Kundalini, in which the practitioner feels a state of oneness and inner peace

Pacihaya: The absorption stage of Kundalini awakening, the stage after Ghata

Prana: The life force that sustains the body

Pranayama: The practice of controlling and regulating the breath

Saraswati: Goddess of knowledge and creativity, often associated with the Kundalini

Shakti: The feminine divine energy often associated with the Kundalini

Svadhishthana: The second chakra, located at the lower abdomen area and associated with emotions

Uddiyana Bandha: Abdominal lock used to draw the Kundalini energy up through the spine.

Vishuddha: The fifth chakra, located at the throat and associated with communication.

Yoga: A set of physical, mental, and spiritual practices used to awaken the Kundalini.

Yoni Mudra: A hand gesture used to help focus the mind, often associated with the practice of awakening the Kundalini.

Yogi: One who practices yoga, meditation, and other spiritual disciplines to cultivate the Kundalini energy.

Conclusion

The ancient, awe-inspiring journey of Kundalini Shakti has been a transformative practice for centuries, connecting individuals to their innermost selves. Every experience is unique, as each person undergoes a different internal transformation. In this process, an awakening of energy is initiated throughout the body. This state brings about profound states of deep meditation and heightened sensory awareness, allowing for great insight into the inner workings of oneself.

The journey can be accompanied by a range of emotions, gradually moving towards greater understanding and acceptance of one's spiritual center. Powerful transformations such as these remind each individual to reach deep within and discover a greater purpose connected with their soul.

Identity is an ever-evolving process that changes as we grow and experience life. As one develops a stronger understanding of themselves, expectations from the outside world seem much less significant. This can be difficult but immensely rewarding as we learn more about our own needs and desires. We become more in tune with what brings us the most fulfillment, accepting our whole self so that we may become present in life with a newfound sense of understanding and empowerment.

Kundalini Shakti is a dynamic energy source that is an energetic guide for individuals seeking self-awareness and personal growth. It is often found within the depths of the unconscious mind, prompting bold exploration that can lead to a discovery of one's true identity and purpose. Those with an open mindset willing to listen to their inner voice and explore the unseen realms within can make great strides towards understanding themselves and their paths. Kundalini Shakti encourages deep contemplation and introspection, offering insight into energy centers hidden away in the depths of the soul that can help one decipher even the most mysterious paths in life.

This guide served as an introduction to Kundalini Shakti and its potential for promoting personal growth and enlightenment. The preceding chapters have discussed the importance of understanding one's chakras, preparing for Kundalini meditation, and learning the essential tools to unlock the energy within. The benefits of awakening this powerful energy and how it can help us on our journey to understanding ourselves have been explored. The four stages of Kundalini energy, Arambha, Ghata, Pacihaya, and Nishpatti, were each explored in depth.

Ultimately, we were reminded that each of us has the potential to tap into the power within, and Kundalini Shakti can serve as a reliable source for unlocking our greatest potential. With a deeper understanding of self and a greater awareness of our spiritual realm, we can begin to take the first steps toward unlocking true power and potential within ourselves. Welcome to the journey of Kundalini Shakti! May it be full of joy and revelations.

Here's another book by Mari Silva that you might like

Your Free Gift
(only available for a limited time)

Thanks for getting this book! If you want to learn more about various spirituality topics, then join Mari Silva's community and get a free guided meditation MP3 for awakening your third eye. This guided meditation mp3 is designed to open and strengthen ones third eye so you can experience a higher state of consciousness. Simply visit the link below the image to get started.

https://spiritualityspot.com/meditation

References

15 signs you're having A Kundalini awakening + what it means. (2021, May 18). Mindbodygreen. https://www.mindbodygreen.com/articles/kundalini-awakening

Cuncic, A. (2019, May 29). How to practice Kundalini meditation. Verywell Mind. https://www.verywellmind.com/what-is-kundalini-meditation-4688618

Isaacs, N. (2021, May 4). Is a Kundalini awakening safe? Yoga Journal. https://www.yogajournal.com/yoga-101/types-of-yoga/kundalini/kundalini-awakening/

Kundalini meditation: Benefits, how to try, and dangers. (2020, August 18). Healthline. https://www.healthline.com/health/kundalini-meditation

Kundalini yoga 101: Everything you wanted to know. (2018, March 16). Mindbodygreen. https://www.mindbodygreen.com/articles/kundalini-yoga-101-everything-you-wanted-to-know

Kundalini: Awakening to the treasure within. (n.d.). Sadhguru.org. https://isha.sadhguru.org/us/en/wisdom/article/kundalini-awakening

Understanding the chakras and Kundalini energy. (n.d.). Art Of Living (India). https://www.artofliving.org/in-en/understanding-chakras-and-kundalini-energy

You are being redirected. (n.d.). Ananda.org. https://www.ananda.org/meditation/meditation-support/articles/awakening-kundalini

www.ingramcontent.com/pod-product-compliance
Lightning Source LLC
Chambersburg PA
CBHW051847160426
43209CB00006B/1188